## What others ai
### *The Power of Pi*

"If you want to experience the life-changing power of God's glorious presence through corporate prayer, then this book is for you."

—Tony Evans

"Oliver Price provides us with practical insights and strategic benefits of corporate prayer, plus a challenge to elevate your prayer life from request-centered to Christ-centered."

—Don Hawkins

"I highly recommend this practical and biblical how-to book for any team of believers serious about accessing divine power in human lives."

—Howard G. Hendricks

"This book is written with passion, a burning desire God has given Oliver Price to rekindle the fire of prayer in our homes and churches."

—Erwin W. Lutzer

"Praying can become routine and we can easily use the same phrases and clichés. Oliver gives instruction that teaches a group of believers to pray expecting the present and listening Lord to do something!"

—Pastor Ken Rogers

"Price has dealt with the greatest need of the church today . . . I commend this book to all those desiring to be men or women of prayer."

—Sammy Tippit

"The usual prayer gathering seems dull and boring to many . . . This book shows us how to pray biblical prayers that exalt Christ and claim His power to bring people into harmony with God and one another."

—Elmer Towns

# The POWER of PRAYING Together

*Experiencing Christ Actively in Charge*

# OLIVER W. PRICE

kregel
PUBLICATIONS

Grand Rapids, MI 49501

*The Power of Praying Together: Experiencing Christ Actively in Charge*

Published by Kregel Publications, a division of Kregel, Inc., P.O. Box 2607, Grand Rapids, MI 49501. Kregel Publications provides trusted, biblical publications for Christian growth and service. Your comments and suggestions are valued.

For more information about Kregel Publications, visit our web site at: www.kregel.com

Cover design: Frank Gutbrod
Book design: Nicholas G. Richardson

**Library of Congress Cataloging-in-Publication Data**
Price, Oliver W.
    The power of praying together: experiencing Christ actively in charge / by Oliver W. Price.
        p.   cm.
        1. Prayer groups—Christianity. 2. Prayer—Christianity.
I. Title.
BV287.P75        1999        248.3'2—dc21        99-24711
                                                                    CIP

ISBN 0-8254-3552-8

Printed in the United States of America

1 2 3 4 5 / 03 02 01 00 99

# Contents

**Fifth Key: Bringing Us into Harmony with Our Father in Heaven**

**Conclusion**

# Foreword

THIS BOOK IS WRITTEN for the spiritually hungry, namely, those who are eagerly seeking a walk with God that will bring joy, peace, and satisfaction. Be prepared to have your heart as well as your mind challenged. If you can read this book without tears, without asking, "How does this relate to me?" and without responding, it should be obvious that you are not really seeking answers.

This book pierces through the veneer of the self-satisfied life, the shallow Christian, the one who is quite content to have little when he or she could have much. It is a book that should be read by pastors and by those to whom they minister, by church leaders who may find that they are not leading as they should, and by all who hunger and thirst after righteousness. This book will bring revival, new comprehension of the potential that lies in every Christian, and constructive answers to the searching question of what really makes life worthwhile.

If you read this book and let it speak to you, it will result in a change in your prayer life, a profound sense of what God has richly provided, and an awareness that those who seek will find.

Dr. John F. Walvoord

# Acknowledgments

I WANT TO EXPRESS MY heartfelt thanks to my wife, Betty. This book has grown out of my prayer partnership with her. We have shared the joy of experiencing the power of Christ in our marriage. The loyal support of our four children and fourteen grandchildren has also been a pillar of strength.

The steadfast prayer support of the board of directors of Bible Prayer Fellowship (BPF), a seventy-year-old prayer ministry of which I am General Director and Minister at Large, helped keep me at it. One member of our board, Joe Humrichous, pastor of Calvary Baptist Church of Danville, Illinois, invited me to teach this vision of Christ-centered prayer to his congregation three times. Then he kept asking me about finishing the book until at last it was done. Another member of our board, Rick Hulkenberg, helped me to edit the forerunner of this book, The Leader's Guide for *Praying with Christ Obviously Present and Actively in Charge,* and printed it for BPF.

My congregation, Metrocrest Bible Church, helped me along by freely joining with me in praying with Christ obviously present and actively in charge. Together we are enrolled in the school of Christ to learn more and more about the blessings of His active leadership.

Craig Claybrook, along with Gary and Karen Cook, gave valuable help in editing this book. Craig and Gary helped me to sharpen its focus, and Karen did the final rewrite of the questions for review. Luella Stolebarger and Kathleen McLarnon have faithfully assisted me with secretarial work. Carlos Flores, Russ Ferguson, Steve Alston, and Lu-Dell Diebold rescued me many times when I just could not make the computer do what I wanted. Wayne Christianson, Editor Emeritus of *Moody Magazine*, helped me to write for *Moody*, and he was a great encouragement in the early stages of giving birth to this book.

Chapters 10 and 11 were originally published in *Moody Magazine* and have been only slightly changed for use here. Portions of chapter 9 were part of an article that I wrote for *Moody*.

If I have failed to name any others who helped, please forgive me. Above all, I give thanks to our marvelous Lord, who has so wonderfully helped me. To Him alone be all the glory!

# IDENTIFYING THE NEED

*Behold, I stand at the door and knock. If anyone hears My voice and opens the door, I will come in to him and dine with him, and he with Me. (Rev. 3:20)*

# Praying with Christ Obviously Present and Actively in Charge

"I've never been in a prayer meeting like that before!" exclaimed the young deacon. The conference in Dallas had ended, and the deacon, along with others, was rejoicing over a life-changing prayer meeting as he was about to return home.

Two couples from the Oklahoma City area and three men from Corpus Christi, Texas, had been deeply moved by messages from Bill McLeod of Canadian Revival Fellowship and Erwin W. Lutzer, Senior Pastor of Moody Church. The two couples approached me and asked, "How can we make this type of spiritual dynamic real in our churches back home?"

"I really don't know what to tell you," I replied, "but I suggest that we get together for prayer. We will ask the Lord Jesus Christ Himself to meet with us and actively take charge. Then you can get your friends back home to join you in claiming the presence and leadership of Christ in your church." The couples responded, "That's good. We usually just assume those things."

A short time later, we gathered in the pastor's study for prayer. I looked around and saw that we were a rather unusual prayer group. The women normally outnumber the men, but we had seven men and three women. There was also a generation gap. My wife, Betty, and I, along with the other couples, were seniors, while the three men from Corpus Christi were baby boomers.

I was pleasantly surprised to see that Sam (not his real name), a young single who lives in Dallas, had joined us. Our differences

11

didn't matter. We all came together in one accord. I began by
reading our Lord's promise to meet with us.

> Again I say to you that if two of you agree on earth
> concerning anything that they ask, it will be done for
> them by My Father in heaven. For where two or three
> are gathered together in My name, I am there in the
> midst of them. (Matthew 18:19–20)

Then I asked, "Can we all agree to base our prayers on four
basic truths in the light of this passage and other related Scriptures? Let me explain. First, we need to *claim the presence of
Christ* in our midst, expecting Him actually to be present by His
Spirit, as He promised. Second, we need to *trust Christ to take
charge* of us because He is the Head of the church. Third, in
practical terms, are we completely willing for Christ to *change
each one of us* as He sees fit? Fourth, are we willing to allow
Christ to *bring us all into harmony* with the Father and thus into
harmony with one another?"

I paused and added, "Now, I want each of you to carefully
consider whether you can heartily agree to unite in prayer on
the basis of these four commitments (namely, to claim Christ's
presence, to trust Him to take charge, to change us as He sees
fit, and to bring us into harmony with the Father and with one
another). I want you to feel perfectly free to say that you are
not ready to accept this basis for our time of united prayer."

After the group thought this through for a moment, they all
agreed and we began to pray. We had barely begun when Sam's
prayer dissolved into tears. For some time, he sobbed as if his
heart would break.

Finally, I asked, "Can we help you?" "I've been away from
the Lord a long time," Sam confessed, "and I want to come back
to Him. Last night, Dr. Lutzer told how Israel had backslidden
and become like a marred clay vessel. God had to break His
people and mold them into a new vessel. I knew that God was
speaking to me and calling me back to Himself."

We were sobered but delighted to see God working in our midst. After we encouraged our brother, we resumed our praying with a sense of great awe and wonder. The Lord had remarkably answered our prayer for His presence and active leadership. By the time we finished praying, all of our hearts were softened because we had drawn closer to the Lord.

Upon leaving, Gene Constantine, the young deacon, remarked, "I've never been in a prayer meeting like that before." What made the difference? Christ was obviously present and actively in charge. We truly had opened the door and invited Him to come into our prayer meeting. In the process, Jesus glorified Himself and met our needs in a marvelous way.

This is not what people usually expect when they pray together. Yet Christ's obvious presence and the freedom our faith and love gave Him to actively take charge are necessary, especially if we want to experience the abundant blessings of the new life we share under His headship.

This is true because Christ is not only *my* life and *your* life, but He is also *our* life. He alone is our living Head, and we are members of His body, the church (1 Cor. 12:12–27; Eph. 1:22–23). Jesus is the tie that binds us to His Father and to one another. When we come together in Christ's powerful presence, He transforms our lives and enables us to keep our unity as fellow members of His body.

Christ has given believers a *new kind* of shared life. "For you died, and your life is hidden with Christ in God" (Col. 3:3). Together with one accord in prayer we advance under Christ's active headship toward our glorious future. "When Christ who is our life appears, then you also will appear with Him in glory" (v. 4).

We are being perfected in unity and purity to be presented to Christ as His bride (Eph. 5:25–27). Small groups, families, and churches are sharing in this powerful work of grace, especially as they unite in prayer with Christ obviously present and actively in charge.

The obvious presence and active leadership of Christ in our homes and churches has always been essential. Just as Jesus must save individual Christians from bondage to the world, their own sinful flesh, and the Devil, so also He must be invited to take charge of couples, fellowship groups, and churches. Christ's preeminent presence and active headship are essential both to our private and our shared relationships with God.

## The Desperate Need of the Hour

Today our Lord's obvious presence and active leadership are more desperately needed than ever before. The angelic messenger to Daniel declared, "And there shall be a time of trouble, such as never was since there was a nation" (Dan. 12:1). In his book significantly entitled *Raising Lambs Among Wolves: How to Protect Your Children from Evil,* Mark Bubeck commented, "These prophetic words from the angelic messenger to Daniel and to us have a message for our times. The troubles upon the nations of the world are mounting up like nothing that has ever been. There seem to be few voices that would dispute the mounting evidence of world chaotic trouble."[1]

Paul warned, "But know this, that in the last days perilous times will come" (2 Tim. 3:1). Surprisingly, the folks that make these last days so perilous are "having a form of godliness but denying its power" (v. 5). We face plenty of attacks from a godless world, but our greatest threat might be from professing Christians who have only a superficial relationship with God and genuine believers. Some young demonstrators in the sixties carried signs saying, "Jesus Yes! Christianity No!" A form of Christianity detached from the obvious presence and active control of the Lord Jesus Christ can be dangerous to our spiritual health!

The usual dull prayer meeting is not preparing Christians for these perilous times. Many believers long to see this changed. A lady told her women's class, "In our Sunday school class of three hundred, whenever we turn our attention to prayer, the requests are all related to people's health. Since the class consists mostly of older adults, this is a valid concern. But there are other deep needs—personal needs—that never get mentioned. It seems that health needs are the only socially acceptable prayer requests we have." One pastor referred to this phenomenon as "the organ recital."

Each week, churches across America schedule midweek prayer meetings. Attendance is meager, at best. Usually, it's the "old guard" who shows up. Prayers seem sincere, yet ineffectual. Board meetings at local churches consist of business item after business item. The meeting may open in prayer. It may even close in prayer. But prayer seems to play a minor role, not only in the board meeting, but also in the overall agenda of the church (even in strong, biblically-based churches).

What's wrong with the usual prayer meeting? What's wrong with our view of prayer itself? What's wrong with us? The believing community desperately needs to redefine the prayer meeting and prayer. Instead of an "organ recital," the urgent need of the hour is to unite in claiming the powerful presence of Christ.

### Christ alone can restore what is missing.

The church has lost its awe of what is *holy*. We have become a mirror image of our society, which is mired in every conceivable sin. The percentage of Christian marriages ending in divorce is about the same as that among the unsaved. Pornography is rampant in the homes of church members. An epidemic of sexual immorality plagues the church. Unrepentant homosexuals are becoming church leaders. Abortion is common. Statistically, one in four women in our pews has had an abortion. A nineteen-year-old girl once asked Dr. James Dobson the profound question, "With all the broken marriages and heartaches, is it worth it to get married?"

### Christ alone can cleanse and renew.

Christians have lost their love for one another. We are fragmented, cut off from other believers over minor doctrinal differences, over race, and over social class *outside* our four walls. Worse still, we are cut off from ourselves *within* our churches.

We maintain superficial relationships, present a veneer of social acceptability, and seldom reveal our true selves. As such, we are lukewarm, impotent, and lacking power.

### Christ alone can breathe His own compelling love into the church.

Churches are splitting apart in alarming numbers. One source estimates that ten thousand churches in North America "split" each year. Unfortunately, many of these are supposedly "solid, evangelical" churches. One missionary went to the field supported by seven churches. Four of these suffered such devastating splits they could no longer continue their support. One of these churches dwindled to only twenty members in their $3 million facility.

### Christ alone can unite us as one body under His headship.

The church has lost its distinctiveness when it comes to ethics. In the American church community, our ethics are about the same as the unbelieving world. A Gallup poll revealed some staggering results:

> While religion is highly popular in America, it is to a large extent superficial; it does not change people's lives to the degree that one would expect from their level of professed faith. In ethical behavior, there is very little difference between the churched and unchurched.[2]

Gallup concluded, "From our surveys, we have found that only about ten percent of the population have what we call "transforming faith."[3]

### Christ alone can bring to life what is dead or dying.

A modern-day prophet sums up the matter by nailing the problem to the wall:

During the present time of moral and spiritual declension, the church is daily losing ground to the world. Each false convert that is added to an already adulterated work adds to the decline and hastens its pace. We have already reached the point where the negative impact of those who profess to be Christians and either are not or are badly backslidden is greater than the positive impact of those who profess to be Christians and truly are. Thus, the church is going backward instead of forward.[4]

**Christ alone can heal and revive the American church.**

We can pretend our problems don't exist or, perhaps, deal with the fallout, one nagging problem at a time. What we really need is to change the way we think and operate.

The time is ripe for the mighty work of God in transforming the church and Christianity as we presently know it. The remarkable success of Henry Blackaby's *Experiencing God* points the way toward the crux of the problem and its solution: *intimacy with God.* Nowhere is this more apparent than in the corporate prayer life of the church and the individual prayers of its members.

The stage is set for an extraordinary renewal of life-transforming prayer meetings in the church and at home. There is growing hunger today for prayer that deeply changes lives and brings people into intimacy with God. The proliferation of the American prayer movement in recent years provides astounding proof of a hunger to get closer to God.

When the Gallup organization did research on the prayer habits of people, they discovered this need, this inner longing for life-changing prayer partnership with God. As news of their survey spread across the country, letters began flowing into their offices asking questions, such as:

1. Is prayer changing me?
2. Is prayer making any difference in my life?

3. Is my prayer life bringing me closer to God?
4. Am I moving toward giving control of my life to God?
5. Do I consistently try to tune in to God's presence?
6. Are my prayers helping me deal with my own sense of self-worth?
7. Are my prayers helping me develop a more loving relationship with others?[5]

Writers Poloma and George Gallup Jr. observed the following:

> The true measure of prayer is whether it transforms the old self into the new self, and changes the way we relate to others. . . . *If we allow God the opportunity to come into our private worlds bringing with Him the good news of His personal love, we will never be the same. His love will change us.* We are reminded that coming to God need not be a complicated task. We need only recognize that God is near, seeking to lead and empower us. (emphasis added)[6]

Prayer is much greater than bringing a list of requests to God. Prayer is letting Jesus Himself come into our midst to commune with us and glorify His name through meeting our needs. Our Lord's heart cry is evident in Revelation 3:20, "Behold, I stand at the door and knock. If anyone hears My voice and opens the door, I will come in to him and dine with him, and he with Me." O. Hallesby, in his classic book entitled *Prayer*, commented as follows:

> I doubt that I know of a passage in the whole Bible that throws greater light upon prayer than this one does. It is, it seems to me, the key which opens the door into the holy and blessed realm of prayer.[7]
> *To pray is nothing more involved than to let Jesus into our needs.* To pray is to give Jesus permission to employ His powers in the alleviation of our distress.

> To pray is to let Jesus glorify His name in the midst of
> our needs. (emphasis added)[8]

The purpose of this book is to explore the full meaning of inviting the Lord Jesus Christ to come into our homes, our fellowship groups, and our churches, and to make His presence and active leadership preeminent. My great burden and desire is for Him to glorify Himself in these settings throughout America.

Am I saying that we do not already pray? No. Most Americans say that they do pray privately. A *Life* magazine survey indicated, "Nine out of ten Americans, ignoring speculation that God is dead, pray frequently and earnestly—and almost all say God has answered their prayers."[9] Gallup polls for over four decades have confirmed this observation.[10] However, the vast majority pray only privately. An Akron Area Survey makes this point:

> Most personal prayer seems to be a solitary activity.
> Sixty-two percent of prayers in A.A.S. had never
> prayed informally with family members, church
> members, or friends; only fourteen percent did so
> regularly.[11]

Private prayer is necessary. But we also need to pray with others, striving to unite under the headship of Christ and His shepherd care. Praying with others in His presence under His active leadership is also necessary. A lady known for her fervent prayers said, "That's where the power is." Another lady commented, "We need to listen to one another's hearts in the presence of God."

Certainly, we need the power of God's Spirit breathing in and through us as we pray. Praying corporately can be structured so as to focus the presence of Christ and unite our prayers under His life-transforming headship. The church began *not as a preaching service* with a small prayer meeting (Acts 1:14); rather, the church *was* a prayer meeting. Armin Gesswein emphasized this significant fact:

> Nor do we read of "the church prayer meeting." The church *was* the prayer meeting. The entire assembly was at prayer. With us, it is not like this. Most of us would not want to belong to a church which does not have a prayer meeting. Neither would we all want to go to prayer meeting. We now have "prayer meeting members" and other kinds of members, a sort of double standard of membership. And this is not being changed, not even challenged! On the contrary, more than one good evangelical congregation is right now wondering what to do with the weak, sick prayer meeting. What is the answer?[12]

The answer is that we must discover the power and blessing of uniting the church and our families in prayer.

## Praying with Jesus Obviously Present in Our Homes

The best place to begin praying is at home. Jesus is knocking on the door of every Christian home, seeking to come in through prayer. He wants to glorify His name through the love, holiness, and unity that He creates in each family. Most of us need assurance that God's high hopes and ideals contained in Scripture can become a reality in our homes. We must somehow "tap into" the presence and power of Christ in our midst.

After I conducted a prayer seminar in Houston, Texas, one mother wrote the following:

> [My] heart's cry for some time has been to see God's order established in our home and to see our family become a family of prayer and unity. . . . Near the beginning of the morning you made a statement that hit me between the eyes. I copied it down quickly and

have referred to it many times this week. You said, "God is able to fulfill your highest hopes and accomplish for you the brightest ideal His Word sets before you." God's peace has come over our marriage and our home this week and I praise Him for His work!

What kind of *hope* does Christ bring when He comes into a Christian home? Our confident hope is that Jesus will unite us in sharing His unity of love with His Father. This is the kind of hope that becomes *visible* to the watching world.

"Impossible," you say. "Utterly unrealistic. No family can rise to such oneness of spirit." Such an attitude forgets the power that Christ brings into our midst. Jesus' words remind us, "For with God nothing will be impossible" (Luke 1:37). In John 17:11–23, Jesus prayed five times for those who follow Him, "that they may be one just as We are one" (v. 22).

Was Christ glibly asking for unity among His followers, knowing full well that it would never happen in this world? Not at all! Jesus prayed, "that they all may be one . . . that the world may believe" (v. 21). Our unity is the instrument in God's hands that awakens people in the kingdom of death and darkness and moves them into the kingdom of life and light. Clearly, Jesus expected this prayer would be answered.

In the book of Acts, this unity began with praying "with one accord" (4:24). Notice what happened after their prayer.

And when they had prayed, the place where they were assembled together was shaken; and they were all filled with the Holy Spirit, and they spoke the Word of God with boldness. Now the multitude of those who believed were of one heart and one soul; neither did anyone say that any of the things he possessed was his own, but they had all things in common. (vv. 31–32)

Though this passage has been warped and twisted by some to argue the case for communism, they miss the point entirely.

Our Lord came into the midst of the young church through prayer. An amazing oneness of love took place (like the oneness enjoyed by the Father and Son). The result? "Great grace was upon them all" (v. 33).

Materialism gave way to unparalleled generosity. This certainly included the couples and families in this community of new believers. Christ likewise comes into our midst today in answer to our prayers to accomplish His will.

Smokey John Reaves, a respected Christian barbecue chef here in Dallas, is also a dynamic lay preacher. He describes how Christ came into his home and made His presence obvious in answer to prayer. "One evening at bedtime, I was deeply burdened and made an unusual request of my wife. 'Gloria, pray with me.' 'No way!' she replied. So I knelt, and while she listened, I prayed, 'Lord, I don't love my wife as Christ loved the church. I don't know how. But if you will teach me, I will.' With that I went to bed and fell asleep. About three in the morning, I was awakened by her weeping. We've been praying together ever since."

Later, Gloria presented John with a new Bible. Inside, I saw this beautiful tribute which says, "I thank God that, through His Word, you have developed into the husband and father that He has ordained from the foundation of the earth. Your willingness to submit to God's will has resulted in spiritual maturity, family leadership ability, and a multitude of blessings for your household. We love you."

God has richly blessed the Reaves' family through prayer and intimacy with Him and one another. Of course, prayers are not always answered so quickly. You may have to be patient and persistent. We can all be encouraged, however, to know that when we open the door to our Lord, He enters into Christian families to unite them in love and holiness.

When concerned individuals have united in seeking the Lord in earnest prayer, they have seen Him wash and cleanse the church and iron out its wrinkles (Eph. 5:26–27). Then the Lord fills the church and its families with His life, manifesting Himself to the lost and dying world through them.

*Our Lord's action in the unsaved world is in proportion to His freedom to act in and through the believing community.* This principle is seen in John 16:7–10, where Jesus promised to send the Holy Spirit to believers, and added that when the Spirit came to them, He would convict the world of sin, righteousness, and judgment. Interestingly, this is what happened in a small, Midwestern town.

## How Christ Came to America's Drug Capital

In 1987, Paul Harvey announced on his news program that Alliance, Nebraska had the highest per capita incidence of drug use in America. But then God intervened! In late 1988, a small group of pastors banded together and poured out their hearts to the Lord. They prayed intensely over a period of fifteen months.

Then it happened. In 1990, God began a powerful work in the churches of Alliance. The breakthrough came on March 18, 1990, when an evangelistic series led by Don Anders stretched far beyond its original eight-day time frame. During those nine and a half weeks, more than nine hundred people out of a population of ninety-five hundred came forward at the meetings to confess Jesus as Lord and Savior of their lives. Every living soul knew that God was at work in their midst.

Powerful, reconciling love changed lives. One man had divorced his first wife and married another. The ex-wife and second wife had experienced eight years of bitterness and sleepless nights. During the meetings, they publicly forgave each other and embraced one another.

A thirty-three-year-old woman and her husband were in the midst of a divorce. He was seeing another woman. Their two daughters were distraught over their parents' sins. The mother committed her life to Christ on March 30 and her family was wonderfully transformed. She later testified about God's intervention:

> God has saved my marriage and family and has put a
> love in my heart and soul, more intense than it has

ever been. God gave me the power of forgiveness, compassion, understanding, love, and control over my
weak human will and thoughts. I could not change,
no matter how hard I tried. I can do nothing. But with
Jesus, anything and everything is possible. I desperately want everyone to know this, that through Jesus
Christ, you can live a first-rate life on earth and have
eternal life in heaven. [13]

One man had a very strained relationship with his mother.
They hardly spoke to each other. The pastor describes their situation this way:

When the meetings began, the family issued a prayer
request for the mother. She came to the meetings and
trusted Christ. The son and his mother embraced in
front of the congregation. Not only did she accept
Christ, but they were completely reconciled and the
bitterness was gone. Shortly afterwards, the man's
wife said, "It's just unbelievable to get birthday cards
and phone calls from my mother-in-law. That hadn't
happened before."[14]

A suicidal woman, who was in the process of divorce, walked
into the meetings and immediately felt the impact of warm love.
That night she trusted Christ for her problems and for eternal
life. The next week, she brought her estranged husband. Together, they joined others in the prayer room, and the next day
they called their lawyers to stop the divorce. This news spread
rapidly and made a huge impact on the whole town.

Seven men spoke during the meetings. According to Anders'
associate, Gene Schupbach, "It didn't matter who spoke or what
they spoke on. People were convicted and went to the prayer
room."[15]

Evangelist Don Anders was quite surprised by such a powerful moving of God. "I don't understand what is happening here,"

he exclaimed, "but it is wonderful."[16] He had never held more than an eight-day meeting in his fifteen years of preaching. He claimed that he had never seen the Holy Spirit work like this before. Jules Ostrander, pastor of Alliance Baptist Church, said, "Preparation for this miracle of God was regular fasting, prayer, and cooperation among pastors."[17]

The secret of this powerful work of God was united prayer. For fifteen months, pastors from five or six denominations prayed together for one hour each week. Daily prayer meetings were held during the crusade. The evangelist spent much time each day fasting and praying. One pastor prayed while the services were in progress. Pastor Sam Reed of the Evangelical Free Church put it this way:

We prayed specifically for renewal of God's people, revival in God's people, purifying of the body, that the body might stand up and be counted, that seeking and hungry people might be drawn where they could hear the Word. We agreed not to pray about any specific personal problems or any particular church problems, but in general for the community that evil would be bound and driven back. *We prayed that God would pour out His Spirit on this community, that sinners would be converted, that the body of Christ would be purified.* (emphasis added)[18]

"The congregations of the participating churches will never be the same," Pastor Reed declared. [19] He concluded:

The thing that has lingered as fruit in the Evangelical Free Church is a new commitment to prayer that I don't think the church had before the meetings. We have a new awareness of what our mission is in this community. People are asking me about learning how to share their faith. We have been giving time to prayer in the Sunday morning worship service in which we break up

into prayer huddles. Lots of people are being prayed
for. It's quiet, but it's continuing. [20]

The good news of Christ's love was on lips everywhere.
Changes took place that no human program could possibly accomplish. Heaven came down, bringing new life and transforming love in astounding proportions!

Can anyone doubt that Christ was obviously present and actively in charge of those churches and families in Alliance, Nebraska? Only Christ could have made such holy cleansing and
heavenly love abound in the drug capital of America.

We are grateful any time we experience a mighty cleansing
and the mending of broken lives. However, let's remember that
the main goal to seek is Jesus' own dear presence. There are
several reasons why it is helpful to specifically pray for the presence of Christ and ask that He will be actively in charge.

First, desperate needs may drive us to seek God's help, but if
that is all we seek, then we have missed the main goal. God's
people have been known to cry to Him for help and then forget
Him after He comes to their aid. Thus after a great awakening,
Christians are prone to enjoy the blessings so much that they
forget the Blesser and drift back into their evil ways.

Second, it is a mark of godliness to seek the Lord (Pss. 42:1;
63:1) and a sign of ungodliness not to seek Him (Rom. 3:11).
God calls people to seek Him and turn from their wicked ways
(Isa. 55:6–7). God rewards those who diligently seek Him (Heb.
11:6). When you love someone, you seek to be with that person. When you no longer desire to be with him or her, your love
has grown cold. Third, Jesus is our life. Our relationships are
spiritually dead if He is not fully present in our lives.

When you claim the obvious presence of Christ, you are
beginning a spiritual journey that will end when you stand
faultless in the presence of God's glory with exceeding joy, which
will endure unbroken forever (Jude 24). This book is designed to
help you and your prayer partners stay close by our Lord on His
highway of holy love until you reach your glorious destination.

There are five keys to effective praying with Christ obviously present and actively in charge. (Originally I focused on four keys, but after further study I saw a fifth.) The first key unlocks the real meaning and purpose of Jesus' presence in our midst. The second key explains the power and real meaning of praying in Christ's name. The third key discloses the great power that is released when we trust Jesus to take charge. The fourth key reveals why and how we must trust Him to change us. The fifth key unlocks the way to enjoy heaven's harmony here on earth. We conclude the book by showing how we can find God, hope, and purpose in the midst of the world's chaos.

## Review Questions

1. What is the current true focus of your church?
   a. Bible knowledge
   b. an emotional charge
   c. living a fulfilling life
   d. programs
   e. building projects
   f. healthy marriages/relationships
   g. Jesus Christ
2. What is the current true focus of your life?
   a. happiness
   b. survival
   c. leisure
   d. accumulation of wealth or possessions
   e. gratification
   f. finding a spouse/family needs
   g. Jesus Christ
3. Does your church currently gather together to pray? If so, what topics are covered?
   a. health, jobs, and church finances
   b. building program
   c. missionaries
   d. brokenness, repentance, and a relationship with Christ

4. Do you agree or disagree with the following statement? Why?

> While religion is highly popular in America, it is to a large extent superficial; it does not change people's lives to the degree that one would expect from their level of professed faith. In ethical behavior, there is little difference between the churched and unchurched.

5. How often and in what situations does your church turn to Christ in united prayer?
6. How often and in what situations do you and your family turn to Christ in united prayer?
7. Which business decisions are dependent on prayer in your church or family?
8. Do you pray with others? If not, why not?
9. What makes you uncomfortable during public prayer?
   a. feelings of inadequacy
   b. never thought about it
   c. too dull
   d. afraid others will use prayer to manipulate me
   e. no one in my social circles prays in groups
   f. I don't know how to pray in a public setting
10. What is the largest group of people (for example, family, church, city, or country) for whom you have prayed?
11. Give an example of when the power of prayer had an impact on your church or family.
12. Read Acts 2:42–47 and 4:32–35. What did the church in Acts have that the modern church does not?
13. In Acts 4:32, materialism gave way to unparalleled generosity. How does your church compare? How do you measure up to this verse?
14. How did the watching world view the church in Acts? How does the watching world view your church? How does the watching world view you?

*Exercises*

1. Set aside a daily/weekly time to pray with your family.
2. Join with them in prayer for your pastor before Sunday services next week.
3. If your church has a weekly prayer meeting, attend it this week.

# THE POWER OF PRAYING TOGETHER: FIVE KEYS

# FIRST KEY:

## CLAIMING THE PRESENCE OF CHRIST

*Then he said to Him, "If Your Presence does not go with us, do not bring us up from here. For how then will it be known that Your people and I have found grace in Your sight, except You go with us? So we shall be separate, Your people and I, from all the people who are upon the face of the earth." (Ex. 33:15–16)*

CHAPTER TWO

# Christ's Powerful, Invisible Presence

In Chapter 1, we saw God powerfully answering the prayers of His people. He displayed His reconciling love in transforming marriages, families, and churches. Perhaps you long to see Christ transform your dearest relationships with His love. You have trusted Christ personally for your eternal destiny, but you know that something is missing.

You may need a revolution in your prayer life. Can you imagine how Jesus' ascension to heaven revolutionized the prayer life of those Christians in the first century A.D.? They prayed in one accord for ten days after His departure (Acts 1:14). What motivated them to devote themselves to prayer for such an extended time? It was their love for Christ. Don't you know that they missed Him? He was their Master, their Savior, their God, and their life. No one had ever loved them as much as He did.

When you love someone, you long to talk to that person, especially when he or she is on a journey. You naturally pick up the phone and talk. Your conversation may go on a long time. Your heart so delights in communing with your lover that you don't notice the clock.

Those first century Christians were drawn to prayer because they loved Jesus. Their prayer was not about a list of things they needed. Their prayer satisfied the hunger of their heart to talk "long distance" with Christ. He was the same Lord Jesus who had walked with them along the shores of Galilee. They saw

Him ascend to heaven, and now they were meeting with Him in prayer. What a delight!

I had a healthy revolution in my prayer life when I quit focusing on a list of items that I wanted to ask God to do and began praying to keep my love relationship with our Lord alive and growing in intimacy. I began to be conscious of His dear presence. Of course, I still ask things from the Lord, but asking for a list of favors is no longer the main concern. Rather, it is enjoying Jesus' presence in the intimacy of love. However, knowing and enjoying conversation with an invisible person is a challenge for most of us. We have to learn to see Christ's invisible presence with the eye of faith.

In this chapter we are going to discover how those first century Christians learned to make the transition from walking with Christ along the shores of Galilee to meeting with Him in one accord in prayer after He ascended to heaven. We will see how Jesus prepared them for this big change.

At the end of the ten days in which the disciples devoted themselves to prayer, the Holy Spirit arrived, and His powerful presence became obvious to both believers and unbelievers alike. He came to take charge as Christ's representative.

In Acts 2, the Holy Spirit came upon this entire assembly of one hundred and twenty disciples with supernatural power. It was then that He filled them with His power (v. 4). The filling of the Spirit resulted in amazing love, unity, and boldness as Jesus' followers witnessed in His name. In chapter 4 we read that a large number had been added to the congregation. In fact, after praying in one accord they were all filled again with the Spirit, and the same amazing grace was upon them all just as on the Day of Pentecost.

The Spirit came upon the church, which is Christ's living body. *The Holy Spirit is ready today to fill the church, including its marriages, families, and small groups. He is not only transforming individuals, but also transforming our relationships in Christ.*

It is significant that this promise of the Spirit coming with power (1:8) was given to an entire assembly of believers and not limited to their leaders. In the Old Testament, the Spirit came in power, primarily upon Israel's leaders. For example, He came upon certain judges and gave them supernatural power to fulfill their God-given mission of delivering Israel from bondage (Judg. 3:10; 6:34; 11:29; 13:25; 14:6, 19; 15:14).

But on the Day of Pentecost the coming of the Holy Spirit upon the assembled church created a new kind of Christ-centered community (Acts 2:41–47; 4:23–35). The church witnessed with such boldness and supernatural power that multitudes were saved. In fact, an idolatrous, pagan society was turned upside down (17:6; 19:18–27).

## Preparation for Jesus' Powerful Presence

Christ carefully prepared His followers for the Spirit's coming. Jesus told them where the Spirit was coming from, where to wait for Him, and what to expect from Him. In Luke 24:49, Jesus explained, "Behold, I send the Promise of My Father upon you; but tarry in the city of Jerusalem until you are endued with power from on high."

Soon after Jesus gave the disciples this promise, He led them out to Bethany. After He had blessed them, He ascended to heaven. Their response to His departure was surprising. They actually "returned to Jerusalem with great joy, and were continually in the temple praising and blessing God" (Luke 24:52–53).

I was shocked when I first noticed this! If I left my flock and they responded with great joy, continually praising God for days afterward, I would conclude that they were glad to get rid of me. This obviously does not explain the great joy of Jesus' followers; so what made them overflow with joy? *Earlier, Jesus taught them that the Holy Spirit would bring them into a wonderful, new relationship with Him.* Instead of being separated from Him, they would share His personal presence and be filled with His resurrection life and power!

In John 14:16–18, Jesus referred to His departure and

promised that He would ask the Father to give the disciples another Helper, who would abide with them forever. This Helper is the Holy Spirit, and He is coequal with the Father and the Son as God. By means of the Spirit, Jesus would actually dwell in the disciples. Thus, Christ would not leave them as orphans. Think about it! Their spiritual union with Christ would parallel the intimacy of His own union with the Father (v. 20).

This new relationship with Christ by means of the Spirit was so much better than before! We now know that it was to the disciples' advantage for Jesus to go away (16:7). His departure and the arrival of the Spirit enabled them to do greater works than Jesus did while He was here on earth (14:12). For example, while the Savior's ministry was confined mostly to Palestine, the apostles preached everywhere and saw the conversion of thousands. Their witness was powerful because the Holy Spirit convicted the world of sin, righteousness, and judgment (John 16:8–11). Furthermore, the Spirit led the disciples into knowing the fullness of all spiritual truth (v. 13).

It's no wonder that the disciples rejoiced when the Lord Jesus Christ departed. They returned to Jerusalem, fully expecting the Holy Spirit to unite them with Christ and reproduce the power of His life in them!

If you took piano lessons from an expert sitting beside you, you might get discouraged. You would know that you could never reach his or her level of skill. What a difference it would make if the spirit of the greatest pianist of all time could enter your body and impart his or her nature and skill to you!

This is similar to what Jesus promised. The Holy Spirit would indwell His disciples and manifest the power of Christ in them! The Spirit would also unite them under the headship of Christ. Because they knew Jesus extremely well, they naturally were ecstatic with joy while waiting for the Spirit to come and endue them with power. They wanted to become more like Jesus.

The disciples knew Jesus as perfect God and perfect man. He is holy, harmless, and undefiled (Heb. 7:26). They had never known a person who lived and breathed in the perfect image and likeness of God. They were impressed with Jesus' great wisdom, His pure love, and His amazing humility. He actually got down on His knees and washed their feet, knowing that they were too proud to perform this duty themselves (John 13:1–16). He gently rebuked them when they argued over which of them was the greatest (Luke 22:24–27). Jesus' ear was always open to their cry. He slept in the boat undisturbed by the noise of a raging storm. But when they cried for help, He instantly awoke and calmed the storm (Mark 4:35–41).

Christ lived His beautiful life of intimate fellowship with God the Father through prayer. Jesus loved and glorified God in all He did, especially in His prayers (John 17:4). He was in the habit of rising early and going to a solitary place to pray (Luke 6:12). He won the greatest battle of His life by persistent prayer in the garden of Gethsemane (22:44).

Christ's love for the disciples did not fail even though they forsook Him while He was on trial for His life (Matt. 26:31). They learned that He loved them enough to die the cruelest form of death for their sake. He sacrificed Himself on the cross to save them from sin and eternal punishment. Jesus was also kind and forgiving. In fact, He loved His disciples and restored them to service after His resurrection. It's no wonder that they waited with great joy for the Spirit to come with power to transform them into the likeness of Christ!

The disciples' longing to be like Christ intensified because they saw themselves as desperately needing a new kind of life. They knew that His obvious presence and active leadership could make the big change needed in their lives.

Those waiting followers were broken people. Before the arrest of Jesus and His subsequent trial, they were self-centered power-grabbers who wanted the elite positions in Christ's kingdom. They were self-confident, self-reliant, and filled with their own courage and strength. They boastfully claimed that they would remain faithful to Christ, even if it cost their lives, or so they thought (Mark 14:26–31).

The disciples' failure to remain loyal to Christ when He was on trial left them broken. They were devastated because they saw the awfulness of their sin, which went far beyond mere cowardice. They saw the despicable evil and greedy selfishness of their nature in sharp contrast to the pure love of Christ. This realization crushed their proud, self-sufficient, and independent spirits.

The disciples became broken, humbled, and completely dependent on God. Thus, their minds, wills, and hearts were opened wide to welcome the Spirit and let Him completely *take charge*. He alone could enable them to become like the Lord they loved and adored.

But how did the disciples get the faith to trust God for this miracle of grace that transformed their whole assembly? *They were prepared to trust God for the miracle of reproducing the love, power, and devotion of Christ in them because they had seen Him do many other miracles.* He fed the five thousand, healed the sick, raised the dead, and finally, He Himself had risen from the dead.

When the Lord Jesus Christ promised that the Spirit would come upon the disciples and endue them with power from heaven, they were ready. They were prepared to joyfully trust Him with every fiber of their being for this miracle of grace.

## Waiting for Jesus' Obvious, Though Invisible, Presence

After Jesus ascended to heaven, His followers returned to Jerusalem, where they assembled in one place, in one accord, in prayer. They waited ten days for the Holy Spirit to come upon them with power (Acts 1:8). *Assembling in one accord in prayer and waiting on God to fulfill His promise are two important spiritual disciplines. This prepared the disciples to experience life as a new kind of community that was endued with power from on high.*

Raymond Ortlund explained the great importance of the discipline of waiting on God:

After Christ's ascension, the believers did not preach. During the ten days they were together, not one person was healed, not one lesson was taught, not one sermon was preached. They had something else to do: to wait on God, to sit quietly until they had His empowering, His direction. The book of Acts has twenty-eight chapters, but only twenty-seven are "acts" or "action" chapters. First, there is one chapter of dead stop! And without that important time of waiting for the Spirit's fullness, there would have been no Pentecost, no ministry, no book of Acts, no early church. There are seasons when the people of God must seek deliberately to put Him first, to give Him time and attention, to seek His mind and His enabling before they proceed with other activities. If the church is centered on anything, anyone, any doctrine, any project (anything but Christ) it is off balance, off center, which means it's "eccentric."[1]

Waiting for the coming of the Holy Spirit was absolutely necessary. Obviously, Jesus could have delayed His ascension to heaven until the day before the Holy Spirit was scheduled to come. Instead, Jesus provided these ten days of waiting because He knew that His followers had to be prepared for a new relationship with Him and with the Holy Spirit.

The disciples were accustomed to gathering around the Lord Jesus and conversing with Him while He was here in the flesh. This had changed. *Now that Jesus Christ was at the right hand of God the Father, they had to learn the discipline of gathering to meet Him in one accord in prayer. They had to wait upon God to send the invisible Holy Spirit to represent Christ on earth.*

The disciples were preparing to enter into the new age of prayer. After Christ's ascension, all believers were given unprecedented freedom to enter the throne room of God in heaven through prayer (Heb. 10:19). Prior to Christ, only the Jewish high priest could enter the holy of holies. Even then, he could only go in one day of the year! Old Testament believers could pray. But they did not have the free, intimate access to God that we now have in Christ (9:6–8).

The significance of this has been illustrated by a story about a former president of the United States. People were waiting in an outer room for their turn to see the president in the Oval Office. A boy walked through the room and directly into the president's office. Waiting visitors were indignant, that is, until they learned the boy was the president's son. Of all the visitors that day, he alone had the intimacy, the free access to his father that only immediate family members could share.

This story may be pure fiction. But it does illustrate our freedom in Christ to enter the throne room of our almighty Father as His children. This is what prayer is all about.

Jesus taught His followers to expect new freedom and power in prayer when He proclaimed, "Most assuredly, I say to you, he who believes in Me, the works that I do he will do also; and greater works than these he will do, because I go to My Father. And whatever you ask in My name, that I will do, that the Father may be glorified in the Son. If you ask anything in My name, I will do it" (John 14:12–14). Christ later said, "Until now, you have asked nothing in My name. Ask, and you will receive, that your joy may be full" (16:24).

Jesus lived on earth and fulfilled His powerful mission by prayer. Now the disciples would share His access to the Father and fulfill their mission by prayer. *They also needed to understand clearly that Christ was still actively in charge of them. He reigned from His seat at the right hand of God and manifested His presence by means of the Holy Spirit, whom He sent.*

This was emphasized all the more by the disciples' waiting until the Spirit came to take charge. As they waited in prayer, they were acting on the basic truth that without Christ, they could do nothing. Jesus told them, "I am the vine, you are the branches. He who abides in Me, and I in him, bears much fruit; for *without Me you can do nothing*" (15:5; emphasis added).

The church, which is on earth, must abide in the love and

intimate fellowship of Christ, who is in heaven. If it does, it will bear much fruit. Otherwise, it will accomplish nothing of eternal value. *Those first Christians discovered the power and authority of uniting together, especially as they waited in one accord in one place in prayer.* Armin Gesswein commented:

> *Assembly-truth is the most powerful truth in the New Testament*, especially as it is on display in the Jerusalem congregation described in the Book of Acts. (emphasis added)[2]

Gesswein also described assembly action as "the new dimension of God's power."[3] Think about the assembly power displayed in Acts 1–2. A small congregation of one hundred twenty despised Galileans assembled in prayer in Jerusalem, where Jesus had been crucified less than two months before. Can you imagine a harder place to preach the resurrection of Christ? Yet their obvious cowardice turned into unbelievable courage!

## Jesus' Powerful Presence in the Assembly

God answers private prayers, but a much greater display of His power is possible when all the members of the church (the living body of Christ) assemble in one accord for a meeting with their Head (Christ Himself) in prayer. Armin Gesswein observed this regarding the powerful church found in Acts:

> The record of it is now divine revelation (telling how much God can do in and with and through even one small congregation). Mass power generates mass production. The new mass is the congregation on fire, and one hundred-twenty members suddenly became 3,120.[4]
>
> Plenary power is reserved for the gathered people of God. Fragmented assembling shreds it. As fire exists by burning, as rain reaches us by raining, so the mighty power of an assembly comes about through assembling.[5]

In one day, three thousand people were converted to Christ and added to the church (2:41). By the fourth chapter, five thousand "men" were added (v. 4). By adding the women and children, there were approximately fifteen thousand new followers of Christ. The power of the Holy Spirit made their assembly beautiful in holiness, unity, and love. As they proclaimed the gospel to a hostile world, they were invincible. They crashed the gates of hell and set multitudes of Satan's captives free. Their opponents panicked (17:6). Their assembly was mighty through the power of God.

This raises a critical question. Is the power of the Spirit so abundantly demonstrated in Acts still available to transform our churches, marriages, families, and small groups today? Is this same Spirit still able to bring transforming power to bear upon a culture and a nation? He certainly is!

We do not need to wait for the coming of the Holy Spirit as the church did in the beginning, but we may need to wait on Him to show us where we have grieved, quenched, or even resisted Him. We can get so busy working for the Lord that we lose the power and blessing of His presence and never even notice!

The New Testament assures us that all the authority and power of our invincible Lord and Savior is still available to us. Consider the words of Jesus in Matthew 28:18–20, which He spoke to His disciples:

> All authority has been given to Me in heaven and on earth. Go therefore and make disciples of all the nations, baptizing them in the name of the Father and of the Son and of the Holy Spirit, teaching them to observe all things that I have commanded you; and lo, I am with you always, even to the end of the age.

It's clear that Jesus is delegating all the authority and power needed by His disciples to fulfill their mission in the world until the end of the age (Acts 1:8).

Paul earnestly prayed that we would be enlightened to understand this important truth when he prayed the following:

> That you may know what is the hope of His calling, what are the riches of the glory of His inheritance in the saints, and what is the exceeding greatness of His power toward us who believe, according to the working of His mighty power which He worked in Christ when He raised Him from the dead and seated Him at His right hand in the heavenly places, far above all principality and power and might and dominion, and every name that is named, not only in this age but also in that which is to come. And He put all things under His feet, and gave Him to be head over all things to the church, which is His body, the fullness of Him who fills all in all. (Eph. 1:18–23)

All the power that raised Christ from the dead and exalted Him to the seat of supreme power is working in us to enable us to be like Christ. With His great wisdom and power, He is washing and cleansing the church so "that [Christ] might present her to Himself a glorious church, not having spot or wrinkle or any such thing, but that she should be holy and without blemish" (5:27). This is enough power to transform Christian marriages and churches into the likeness of the Savior (vv. 22–30).

Christ's intercession will always enable us to live as new people in spiritual union with Him. "Therefore He is also able to save to the uttermost [completely] those who come to God by Him, since He always lives to make intercession for them" (Heb. 7:25). Throughout its history, the church has often drifted away from pursuing a holy life devoted completely to Christ (Rev. 2:1–7). Then some folks begin to pray for God's people to wake up, return to Christ, and claim His mighty power for holy living. Their prayers have been remarkably answered.

## Christ's Powerful Presence in Colonial America

In *A Faithful Narrative of the Surprising Work of God,* Jonathan Edwards told how a great awakening came to his town. He noted that when he arrived in Northampton, Massachusetts, in 1726, he faced "a time of extraordinary dullness in religion. Licentiousness for some years greatly prevailed among the youth in the town."[6] Corruption spread, especially as many young people became indecent in their behavior in church. Parents were ineffective in curbing their children's bad habits. Many church members were not born again.

In the fall of 1734, Edwards started prayer meetings. He also began a series of sermons on justification by faith (and thus not by works). It was "in the latter part of December, that the Spirit of God began extraordinarily to set in, and wonderfully to work among us," Edwards exclaimed.[7] The conversion of a young woman whose evil ways were well known hit the young people and many others "like a flash of lightening."[8]

All at once "a great and earnest concern about the great things of religion and the eternal world, became universal in all parts of town, and among persons of all ages."[9] Many were converted. Edwards comments as follows about the spring and summer of 1735:

> *The town seemed to be full of the presence of God:* it never was so full of love, nor so full of joy, and yet so full of distress (because some were still coming under conviction of sin), as it was then. There were remarkable tokens of God's presence in almost every house. It was a time of joy in families on account of salvation's being brought unto them; parents rejoicing over their children as new born, and husbands over their wives, and wives over their husbands.[10] (parenthesis and emphasis added)

Public worship was enlivened. People sang with grace in their hearts in the beauty of holiness. Christ was present and preeminent, not only on Sunday, but whenever people met together. People who had been converted a long time were now "greatly enlivened and renewed with fresh and extraordinary incomes of the Spirit of God."[11]

This spiritual renewal of the church and its families came in answer to united prayer and in response to Jonathan Edward's strong biblical messages. Within two years, this awakening spread to over one hundred communities along the Connecticut River Valley. It permeated the Northern Colonies, now known as New England, under the leadership of such gifted preachers as Edwards, Backus, and Whitefield. Whitefield also spread revival fires in the Southern Colonies of Georgia and South Carolina. Revival eventually moved to the Middle Colonies of Virginia and North Carolina under the auspices of such leaders as the Tennents and Frelinghuysen.

Schools, which later became universities, sprang up to prepare men for the ministry. Most of the first universities founded in America were established for this purpose, Harvard and Yale included. Revivalists founded Queen's College, now Rutgers University.[12] Gilbert Tennent's "Log Colleges" became the forerunners of modern seminaries.[13] Whitefield helped raise money for the College of New Jersey, later renamed Princeton.[14] He also was instrumental in raising a large sum of money for what became Dartmouth College.[15]

Whitefield was mindful of the social needs of his day, and this is why he established Bethesda Orphanage in Savannah, Georgia.[16] He also demonstrated a high level of interest in public affairs and profoundly influenced Benjamin Franklin.[17] In particular, the preaching of George Whitefield helped to unite spiritually the thirteen colonies and prepared them to join as one nation founded on biblical principles. This new spiritual climate permeated the land and became the seedbed for a new country.

Today we look back at this time in our nation's history and refer to this extraordinary work of God as "The First Great Awakening." The Colonies were radically transformed by the mighty moving of the Spirit of God in the hearts of individuals, churches, and communities throughout the thirteen colonies. How desperately we need the fresh work of God today!

## Review Questions

1. For what purpose did the Holy Spirit come upon leaders in the Old Testament?
2. According to Matthew 28:18–20, how much authority does Jesus have? To whom did He delegate this authority?
3. Acts 1:8 makes a connection between the Holy Spirit and power. What was the primary purpose of this bestowal of God's Spirit and power? What was the intended result?
4. What caused the church to rejoice when Jesus ascended to heaven?
5. For what reason did the Holy Spirit come upon the whole church (Acts 2)? What were believers found doing when the Spirit came? What happened when the Spirit came?
6. How can we claim the same transforming power today, as described in the following statement?

> The power of the Holy Spirit made the disciples' assembly beautiful in holiness, unity, and love. As they proclaimed the gospel to a hostile world, they were invincible. They crashed the gates of hell and set multitudes of Satan's captives free. Their opponents panicked. Their assembly was mighty through the power of God.

7. What advantages have you experienced recently from abiding in the Spirit?
8. According to Ephesians 5:27, why does Christ desire the church to rid itself of any spot, wrinkle, or other moral blemishes? What spots, wrinkles, and blemishes affect the church today?
9. In your personal life, how have you experienced "the discipline of waiting upon God?"

10. What current need causes you to wait upon God?
11. What would you like to see the power of Christ accomplish in your church? In your family?
12. Where have you already seen the transforming power of Christ in your life?
13. How long is too long to wait for God's promises?
14. What groups of people do you interact with that could become a united assembly in prayer?
15. If you want to see God send revival, what must you do? What must the church do?

*Exercises*

1. Share a request for what you would like to see the power of Christ accomplish in your life with at least one other member of your church. Commit to pray with this person weekly until God answers the request.
2. Continue to attend your church's prayer meeting, or meet with others from your church, to pray for the transformation of your congregation and the way its members relate to one another.

## CHAPTER THREE

# Christ: Guest or Resident?

IN JONATHAN EDWARDS'S DAY, the powerful presence of Christ represented by the Holy Spirit brought new life, purity, and love to the church in New England. This is only one of many such occurrences. They are usually called revivals, spiritual awakenings, or renewals.

In any case, a powerful work of the Holy Spirit brings renewed holiness and purity. The Spirit also brings healing and reconciliation to broken relationships. God is obviously present and actively working with amazing grace. Spiritual awakening is born out of a new passion for prayer and is maintained through fervent commitment to God in prayer.

In 1904 and 1905 after much prayer, a mighty work of God's grace swept through Wales in Great Britain. Arthur Wallis told of a meeting near the town of Gorseinon that continued throughout the night. A hardened, godless miner was returning from work at 4 A.M. that morning. Seeing a light in the chapel, he decided to investigate. As soon as he opened the door, he was utterly overwhelmed by a sense of the presence of God. With great surprise to himself and others, he exclaimed, "Oh, God is here!" Afraid either to enter or depart, he stood there at the door, as God's Spirit began melting his heart and bringing the work of salvation to his hardened soul.

Fruit from this renewal continued for years in the changed lives of many individuals. With the passing of time, however, the corporate life of the churches drifted downhill to the old ways of unbelief and selfishness. Today, the churches scattered throughout

Wales need another visitation from God, another awakening from the Lord.

Does it have to be this way? Does the Lord Jesus Christ merely want a temporary visit with His church? Does the church only require the fresh visitation of God when times are desperate and homes are broken? Certainly not!

## Christ Should Obviously Reside in Our Midst

Our Savior, the Lord Jesus, knows that His presence and active leadership are absolutely essential to the spiritual life of our homes and churches. He wants to become a "permanent resident." He promised that He would be in the midst of even two or three who gather together in His name (Matt. 18:19–20).

The assembly of Christians is called to be a dwelling place for God on earth. This is described in Ephesians 2:18–22:

> For through Him we both have access by one Spirit to the Father. Now, therefore, you are no longer strangers and foreigners, but fellow citizens with the saints and members of the household of God, having been built on the foundation of the apostles and prophets, Jesus Christ Himself being the chief cornerstone, in whom the whole building, being fitted together, grows into a holy temple in the Lord, in whom you also are being built together for a dwelling place of God in the Spirit.

After declaring that all believers have access to God in prayer by one Spirit, Paul explains that we are "the household of God" (v. 19). The apostle also declares that our lives are being "built together for a dwelling place of God in the Spirit" (v. 22). Paul prayed, "May Christ through your faith [actually] dwell (settle down, abide, make His permanent home) in your hearts" (3:17, *Amplified New Testament*).

Christ was in the midst of the seven churches (Rev. 1:12–20).

He actively took charge of them. He commended them for their good qualities and also pointed out their sins. He called on them to repent of their corporate sins or face the consequences (chaps. 2–3).

Even in the Old Testament, God was present in the midst of His people. He actively took charge in a special way. God met with the congregation of Israel at the tabernacle. He dwelled in their midst and ruled over them as their God (Exod. 25:22; 29:42–46). God made His presence obvious through the pillar of cloud by day and the pillar of fire by night. His glory hovered over the tabernacle and filled it (40:34–38).

The temple was known as God's dwelling place in later times and served as a special place to assemble for prayer. He proclaimed, "My house shall be called a house of prayer for all nations" (Isa. 56:7).

God's presence in the midst of His people marked them as united with Him as His dearly beloved. As such, they enjoyed His special protection and care. Disobedience and idolatry caused God to withdraw temporarily from the camp of Israel (Exod. 32:1–8; 33:1–10). Moses made a strong plea for God to keep His residence in their midst. He saw God's continued withdrawal as an invitation for disaster. God's presence made the difference between Israel and the pagan nations (33:15–16).

Christ's special presence is, likewise, essential for the life of the church. When He departs from a congregation, it dies. Unfortunately, the dead church does not even know it, just as a pastor once said, "If the Holy Spirit left the church, no one would notice because it runs so smoothly without Him."

At Laodicea, Christ was outside the church. He gave it one final call to repent of its sins or He would disown the congregation and vomit it out of His mouth (Rev. 3:14–22). God looks forward to dwelling among His people forever, when their sins and backsliding ways will never again cause His withdrawal (21:3).

Enjoying the special presence of Christ in our midst, as well as welcoming Him there, ought to be the essential ingredients of our church ministry. The tendency is to wait until the church falls into desperate spiritual need before we wake up and honor the Lord's presence.

The church today needs to purpose in its heart to seek God earnestly, just as Daniel purposed in his heart *not* to defile himself by eating the king's meat (Dan. 1:8). We need to make up our minds by asking whether we want Christ among us. If so, we need to make the Lord Jesus completely at home in our midst, at all times, always. We desperately need to unite in loving, trusting, and obeying Him, for He is our life. Without Him, our homes and churches are spiritually dead.

## Examples of Our Lord Obviously Residing in Churches

Some pastors have led their churches to enjoy consistently the presence of Christ. For instance, Dr. C. John Miller, former professor at Westminster Seminary and founding pastor of New Life Presbyterian Church in Jenkintown, Pennsylvania, held prayer meetings where Christ was obviously present and actively in charge. Because the meeting was *exciting*, attendance grew. When they outgrew the basement, they moved to the auditorium. The lost were frequently saved in answer to prayer. Often, the new believers began attending prayer meeting. The lives of believers were wonderfully transformed.

Ten years earlier, Dr. Miller had served another church and had watched helplessly as his prayer meeting went through death throes and finally died. He concluded upon reflection that he himself had killed it. His great self-reliance had caused him to believe that his preaching and hard work were all that was necessary for success. Consequently, he had given prayer and the active work of the Holy Spirit a minor role, at best.

By the time Dr. Miller started New Life Presbyterian Church, he understood the crucial importance of the prayer meeting. He had learned to depend completely on the Lord in prayer for every aspect of his ministry. He led New Life Presbyterian to do that, too. His book, *Outgrowing the Ingrown Church*, tells how

he prayed for the prayer meeting and saw it develop into a powerful time that gave birth to a church that was alive under the
powerful, active leadership of Christ. With the Lord in charge,
New Life Presbyterian Church grew from a home Bible class to
more than six hundred members. In addition, it sponsored two
daughter churches.[1]

Adoniram Judson Gordon, one of the great men of American
history, lamented his dead church. Like dust, a thick layer of
death covered Clarendon Street Baptist Church in Boston. This
was the fashionable congregation of its time where bankers and
Boston's social elite gathered. A secular, worldly spirit dominated
nearly every aspect of its life. The pews were rented. Unsaved
singers from the opera were hired, and they rendered music as
spiritually dead as the singers themselves.

A deacon dared to print a leaflet that stated, "Strangers welcome." He was promptly rebuked by an elder who said, "You
might get the wrong kind of people in here!" Of course, everyone knew about "the right kind."

Pastor Gordon's heart experienced deep travail, grieving continually over the spiritual condition of his church. Maintaining
the appearance of a "proper" pastor became a heavy load, press-
ing him to the point of desperation. He knew that his people
needed to repent and return to Christ. Therefore, he spent more
time on his sermons. More disappointment followed as few, if
any, were converted even after he spent a week of solid toil in
sermon preparation.

Pastor Gordon could have listed his prayer meeting in the
obituary column of the local newspaper. He thought, "If I could
only get the people together to pray." Yet, in spite of all he could
do, very few attended prayer meeting. Of those few, no one ever
rose to pour out their heart to God for the sad spiritual condition of the church.

About this time, the administration of the church began to
come unglued. Strong opposition developed among some of the
church officers. Pastor Gordon was forced to devote his time and
energy "to get the members to vote as they should." He

anticipated that certain members would help him. Instead, they hindered. Faced with tremendous discouragement, sleepless nights, and pressurized living, he made a trip to the doctor, who prescribed absolute, complete rest as the only remedy.

While struggling to continue in the ministry on such "rocky soil," the pastor fell asleep one Saturday night as he was completing work on his sermon. He had an unusual dream. He was standing in the pulpit, about to preach before a full auditorium when a stranger entered the church. The stranger passed slowly down the left aisle, looking for anyone who would share their rented pew. Halfway down the aisle, a man offered him a place and he quietly accepted. Gordon's eyes were riveted on this visitor. He wondered, "Who can that stranger be?" He determined to find out.

After the sermon, the stranger slipped out with the crowd. The pastor asked the man with whom he sat, "Can you tell me who that stranger was who sat in your pew this morning?" In a most matter-of-fact way, the man replied, "Why, don't you know that man? He is Jesus of Nazareth." Seeing the pastor's great consternation, the man assured him, "Oh, don't be troubled. He has been here today and, no doubt, He will come again."

Gordon was filled with an indescribable rush of emotion and self-examination. Why the Lord Himself was here listening to the sermon today! He asked himself, "What was I saying? Was I preaching on some popular theme in order to catch the ear of the public?" With a sigh of relief, Pastor Gordon remembered that he was preaching Christ. Then his conscience demanded, "But in what spirit did I preach? Was it in the spirit of one who knows that he himself is crucified with Christ? Or did the preacher manage to magnify himself while attempting to exalt Christ?"

For the first time in his life, A. J. Gordon was electrified with the truth that *Christ Himself had actually come to church!* The pastor could never again care what people thought about his preaching or his church. He thought, "If I could only know that Jesus was not displeased, that He would not withhold His feet from coming again because He had been grieved at what might have been seen or heard!"

All of Pastor Gordon's priorities were changed. His life and ministry would never be the same. He fell at the feet of his Lord in worship and turned the administration of the church over to Him. The pastor then taught his board and his people to let the Holy Spirit actively take charge on behalf of Christ.

"Not that I attach any importance to dreams or ever have done so," the pastor wrote. "I recognize it only as a dream; and yet I confess that the impression of it was so vivid that, in spite of myself, memory brings it back to me again, as though it were an actual occurrence in my personal ministry."[2]

Belief that Christ actually does come to church and is ready to take charge transformed Clarendon Street Baptist. The people *let Jesus* take charge. Over a period of eight years, the presence and leadership of Christ became the focal point. The pastor and the leaders genuinely sought the Lord in prayer and the church was wonderfully changed.

Adoniram Gordon replaced the spiritually dead opera singers with lively congregational singing. New life came into the church and the spiritually dead members who refused to repent drifted out. The Lord sent the church an ardent soul winner by the name of Uncle John Vassar. This man shared his vision for evangelism and won many to Christ through prayer and door-to-door visitation.

D. L. Moody built a tabernacle a few blocks from the church. A number of new believers, including ten men addicted to drink, were converted and came to Clarendon Street. "They won't last," the skeptics insisted. But they were wrong. These men and others from Moody's meetings became strong, steadfast Christians.

The church developed an outreach to the ethnic communities in Boston. Missionaries went out to foreign lands. A training ministry began to prepare workers for the harvest.

Christ transformed the ministry of A. J. Gordon and changed Clarendon Street Baptist Church into a powerful spiritual lighthouse that endured for many years. The church literally passed from death to life. It came about as the pastor taught his people the reality of letting Christ come into their midst by the Holy Spirit and actively take charge. Christ is ready today to settle down and make His home with any couple, small group, or church where Christians open their hearts in one accord in prayer to welcome Him.

## Review Questions

1. Spiritual awakening is born out of a new passion for and maintained by a fervent commitment to one thing. What is it?
2. According to Ephesians 2:19–22 and 3:17, where is Christ to make His permanent home?
3. Where did God "reside" in the Old Testament?
4. What did God do when the camp of Israel engaged in disobedience and idolatry?
5. Do you agree or disagree with the following statement? Why?

   If the Holy Spirit left the church, no one would notice His absence, for it runs so smoothly without Him.

6. In what ways is the church today similar to the American culture? In what ways is it not?
7. How has the relationship between believers and their local church changed since the time of the early church?
8. Where are your closest relationships formed and developed—at home, at work, within the family, or at church?
9. What should be the essential ingredients for our church ministry?
10. Do you agree with the following statement about the church? Why or why not?

    The tendency is to wait until the church falls into desperate spiritual need before we wake up and seek the Lord.

11. What ingredient, humanly speaking, causes attendance at prayer meeting to grow?
12. In order to claim the promise of the presence of Christ, what must we purpose to do?
13. What happens if we stop trusting Christ to change us as He sees fit?
14. Can you remember a time when you were consumed with the love and power of Christ, or a time when your family or church was driven by the love and power of Christ? What was most memorable about that time?
15. What are some activities in which you and your family could participate that would rekindle your love for Christ?

*Exercises*

1. Meet with another family in your church and develop a Christ-centered relationship. Share family prayer needs and pray together.
2. Volunteer for an activity in your church and encourage the rest of your family also to volunteer.

CHAPTER FOUR

# Three Dimensions of Christ's Presence

WHEN LEADING A PRAYER meeting in the past, I used to take it for granted that we entered the presence of Christ, but not anymore. Actually, He could have been silent, inactive, or even absent and I would not have noticed. Now I have changed. Whether praying with my wife or leading a prayer meeting, I have learned to recognize the absolute, crucial importance of Christ's presence. Three dimensions of His presence need to permeate our understanding. They are His *universal* presence in the world, His *gracious* presence in the church, and His *glorious* presence in the church.

## The Universal Presence of Christ

During His time on earth, Jesus lived in Palestine. He experienced such things as hunger, fatigue, and pain. When the Son of God rose from the dead, He received a glorified, resurrection body. He now no longer is subjected to the limitations of living on earth in human form. Because Jesus is in heaven at the right hand of the Father, He is everywhere present to help and guide believers.

The term for this is "omnipresence" or "universal presence." It means that Christ is present everywhere at all times. Sometimes His universal presence is obvious to those who are discerning and sometimes it remains hidden and unnoticed. The universal presence of Christ remains true, despite our lack of sensitivity or awareness. He sees everything and, as such, He knows everything. This realization gripped the psalmist as he searched in vain

59

throughout the universe for a place to hide from the presence of God (Ps. 139:1–12).

The sobering realization of Christ's universal presence is understandable but uncomfortable. Many of us know people who are so godly that we try to avoid them for fear that they will see through us and know our weaknesses and sins. For example, some people feel this way about their pastor.

One pastor surprised a couple in his church when he showed up on their front doorstep. Inside he heard, "It's the pastor! Hurry and get rid of the cigarettes. He'll know that we smoke." Of course, the room was wafting in smoke when he entered. Obviously, the husband and wife were uncomfortable because they wanted to put on their "Sunday best" for the pastor.

The psalmist's fear began to change as he thought about the all-powerful, ever-present, all-knowing God, who lovingly watched over him from the time when he was in his mother's womb. The writer's initial impulse to escape the divine presence changed completely into an intense desire to worship God. "I will praise You, for I am fearfully and wonderfully made; marvelous are Your works, and that my soul knows very well" (v. 14). The psalmist continues, "How precious also are Your thoughts to me, O God! How great is the sum of them! If I should count them, they would be more in number than the sand; when I awake, I am still with You" (vv. 17–18).

What an astounding truth! Like a blanket, God's thoughtful care covers us while we sleep! Day and night, God reflects upon all the good things He can do for us! God's loving care goes with us continually, especially as He showers upon us all the heavenly favors that His infinite love can design, and all the eternal goodness that His infinite power can provide.

The psalmist saw that it was dangerous and useless to flee from the presence of God. There was really no place to hide. Furthermore, if he ran from God, he would end up in the way of the ungodly. He might turn out like the prodigal son who left his father and wasted his inheritance on harlots and riotous living (Luke 15:11–16). Or the psalmist could wind up like the prodigal's elder brother, who had just enough self-righteousness and self-centered religion to make him miserable (see vv. 25–30).

In any case, the psalmist faced a "no-win situation." As he meditated on the God of compassion and love, the God whose heart yearned over him day and night, the lure of life alienated from the Lord lost its appeal. The psalmist no longer wanted the isolation and the self-centeredness that such a life dictates.

As the writer's thoughts continued, he burned with passionate zeal for God's honor (Ps. 139:19–22). He enlisted on the Lord's side, choosing to defend Him from the onslaught of the wicked (v. 20). God's enemies became the psalmist's enemies. He recognized that partnership with evil reaped only temporary benefits, but that partnership with God reaped eternal rewards. Thus, he shunned the enemies of the Lord and their wicked ways. Instead of running *from* the presence of God and His all-seeing eye, the psalmist ran *to* God and His everlasting mercy. He made a 180 degree turn, all because he now understood the character and attributes of God.

Since God knew the psalmist better than he knew himself, he asked God to search him and know him. He sought the all-searching eye of God, as well as the all-loving mind of God, to help him discover hidden sins that he was prone to overlook. The writer found renewed vigor as he more fully appreciated a powerful God whose might helped him to forsake every form of evil that hindered his partnership with the Lord (vv. 23–24). Finally, the psalmist asked God to lead him in the only wise direction, namely, "in the way everlasting" (v. 24).

The psalmist came to recognize sin for what it really is—a deadly danger and a despicable disgrace to God. He saw that sinful self-will is like a deadly disease that he needed to remove completely from himself. Only the all-present God could enable him to accomplish so great an endeavor.

A student at a Bible college started to tell a shady joke, but first he asked, "Are there any girls around?" His friend replied, "No. But the Lord is here." Another responded, "He will be offended by anything that offends the girls." The shady joke was cut off. The truth is evident. We may *forget* the presence of Christ but we can never *escape* from it.

How many church fights, family feuds, and immoral acts would occur if we recognized, appreciated, and fully understood the awesome reality of the universal presence of Christ? What would happen if married couples, families, small fellowship groups, and entire congregations waited on God in prayer until the joy, hope, and holiness of Christ's presence was fully realized? They would be transformed like the psalmist.

Believers need to understand and relate to the universal presence of Christ in this way, for God wants us to enjoy His presence in a special love relationship. Many Christians have shared the psalmist's prayer that God would search them. The presence of a perfectly holy God, who is able to set us free from selfishness and sin, ought to be in our praise and prayers. The remembrance of His presence is purifying.

## The Gracious Presence of Christ

Christ's presence in the midst of His church has a different meaning from His universal presence in the world in rebellion against Him (Psalm 2). Unlike the world, the church gathers around Christ in love. He is free to pour out His blessings on the church and to enable it to share the riches of His grace. But of necessity He relates to the world on different terms.

Christ meets His church at His throne of grace (Heb. 4:16). If we sin, we will be chastened, but we will not be condemned with the world (1 Cor. 11:32). Christ gives us the riches of His grace, and is perfecting us in holiness (Eph. 5:25–27). He deals with the rebelling world from His throne of supreme power and authority (1 Tim. 6:15–16). The unsaved must be reconciled to Him or face destruction (Ps. 2:8–9).

Believers should know Christ both as their universal sovereign and as their loving Savior, who seeks to dwell in their midst, reign over them, and share with them His grace and love. When you get to know someone in a loving relationship, you are motivated to share all that you have with this person. Let me give a personal illustration.

Many years ago, there was a young lady named Betty in the youth group where I served as youth pastor. I was in her presence regularly in the role of a minister. She was very active in the group and responded well to my ministry. Things changed when I began to visit her one-on-one for a Bible study. It didn't take long for me to change the sense of my presence with her. I wanted to spend time with her just to enjoy her company. She agreed, and thus I became her suitor. Obviously, the meaning of my presence as her boyfriend was quite different from my presence as her youth pastor. If I had sensed that she was not pleased to have me as her suitor, I would have had to withdraw my presence.

In some ways Christ's presence in the midst of His people is quite similar to that of a suitor. When we view the church as the Bride of Christ, the analogy becomes all the more meaningful. His gracious presence as Head of the church is quite different from His universal presence in the world. Christians can appreciate both His universal presence and His gracious presence.

My presence as Betty's youth pastor continued after she welcomed my presence as her boyfriend. After fifty-plus years of marriage, she knows my presence in two different relationships, namely, as her pastor and as her husband.

Our love has grown more intimate through the years. Intimacy means that we have a very close relationship and great freedom to share our thoughts and all we have with each other. Intimacy also means that we easily recognize one another's moods and feelings. Loving intimacy means that we care about each other's feelings. If we sense that our partner is anxious, wounded, or withdrawn, we show concern. We don't want to coldly stomp on one another's emotions.

Our relationship with Christ is also like that. We seek to be sensitive to anything in our lives that grieves Him or squelches His love for us. God sought intimacy with the psalmist. The Lord

did not want to guide his servant like a stubborn mule who re-
sists his master's directions. God wanted to lead the psalmist in a
reasonable and sensible manner (Ps. 32:8–9). In other words, the
Lord wanted him to be alert to His will and eager to follow it.

There are degrees of intimacy. Consider my marriage to Betty.
I remember the early years when we were just getting accustomed to knowing each other as a couple. Over time, we have
advanced to a high degree of intimacy. In a similar way, there
are degrees of intimacy in our love relationship with Christ. One
of the great purposes of prayer and Bible study is to advance
toward the greatest possible degree of intimacy with our Lord
and Savior.

Christ Himself had "degrees of intimacy" with His followers.
For instance, He had over five hundred followers but chose only
seventy for a closer relationship. Closer still were the Twelve.
Out of these, there were three—Peter, James, and John—who
were members of Christ's inner circle. And John was closest of
all. In fact, he was known as "the one whom Jesus loved" (John
21:20).

Of all Jesus' followers, only one had the spiritual eyes to see
and the discernment to understand that He was about to die.
Only Mary learned from Christ while sitting at His feet. At just
the perfect time, she worshiped Him by anointing His feet with
expensive ointment. In effect, she was anointing Him for His
burial (12:1–7).

In the Old Testament, Moses held the distinction of being one
of God's closest friends of all time. "But since then there has
not arisen in Israel a prophet like Moses, whom the LORD knew
face to face" (Deut. 34:10). For the Lord to know us face to face
requires us to be completely open and honest with Him in His
presence. After Adam sinned, God asked him what he had done
(Gen. 3:11). The Lord was not seeking information. Rather, He
wanted to bring Adam's sin out in the open so that both of them
could look at it together. Then God could give Adam the remedy
for his sin so that the barrier between them would be removed.

A man came to me once seeking spiritual help. I knew what

was wrong. He was addicted to heavy drinking, but I could not get this out in the open. He was not ready to be completely honest with me. So we just talked around the issue. Sadly, he would not let me know him face to face.

We must seek God's face and open ourselves to Him, especially as He seeks to know us face to face. Seeking such intimacy with the Lord is at the heart of a growing prayer relationship with Him. Love for God motivates us to seek His face. When He reaches out to us in intimacy and love, we should gladly respond. "When You said, 'Seek My face,' my heart said to You, 'Your face, LORD, I will seek'" (Ps. 27:8).

There are times when our Lord may hide His face from us because we harbor sin in our hearts. When we refuse to confess and forsake our sin, we spurn His intimate presence as our loving Lord. It requires sensitivity on our part to recognize His withdrawal and lack of intimacy with us. It is God's way of prompting us to find out *why* His intimacy is withdrawn.

The psalmist urges, "Do not hide Your face from me; do not turn Your servant away in anger; You have been my help; do not leave me nor forsake me, O God of my salvation" (v. 9). The Lord had admonished the writer to seek the intimacy of His face (v. 8). The psalmist was painfully aware of the awful dread of losing intimacy with God, who loved him so much!

To maintain this close intimacy with the Savior, we must love and obey Him fervently with all our heart (Rev. 2:4–5). An intimate love relationship requires our wholehearted obedience. Jesus said, "You are My friends if you do whatever I command you" (John 15:14).

Jesus loves us despite our sinful ways. But unconfessed sin raises a barrier to His intimate love. Transgression brings something into our lives that Christ cannot share with us. Mutual, open, and honest intimacy with Christ vanishes until we confess our sin and forsake it.

Maintaining intimacy with God and people is sometimes painful. During our first year of marriage, I was upset with Betty about something so trivial that I don't even remember the exact incident. But I do recall giving her the silent treatment. I had always been a very private person. The idea of a completely transparent relationship with anyone was foreign to me. Despite my efforts to hide my peevishness, she tried to pry open my shell at the supper table.

"Well, what did you do today?"

"Nothing."

"What's wrong with you?"

"Oh, nothing."

"Well, that's an awful lot of nothing. There is something wrong with you. What is it?"

"No! There's nothing wrong."

Whatever was wrong was the size of an anthill. But now it seemed like a mountain. I was embarrassed and even more buried under a pile of stifled emotions. I thought, "Why can't she just leave me alone!" When we finally crawled into bed, I lay there stiff as a board. I wanted Betty to believe that my conscience was perfectly clear. But she wouldn't buy it.

When Betty could take the silent treatment no longer, she poked me in the ribs, demanding, "Are you sleeping or pretending?" With this, I rolled over and told her all my thoughts. We both wept and kissed and fell into a pleasant sleep.

What was going on here? Though it was painful, I learned a lesson in letting Betty know me face-to-face. More importantly, allowing her to know me intimately has helped me immensely in letting the Lord know me face-to-face. Closeness with my wife taught me a great deal about drawing near to God.

Obviously, drawing near to God requires far more heart searching! James wrote, "Draw near to God and He will draw near to you. Cleanse your hands, you sinners; and purify your hearts, you double-minded" (James 4:8). As individuals, married couples, small groups, and churches, we must learn to listen to God's words of loving rebuke, and even seek His exposure of the ways that we grieve Him so that we can maintain a love for Him that holds nothing back.

The tendency is to think that we should confess the "big" sins and ignore the "little" ones. Not so! A small sin can come between us and our Lord just as my "little irritation" came between me and my wife. The sin is serious when it leads us to hide our face from the Lord.

We must unite in abiding in Christ just as branches mutually abide in the vine. This results in fellowship, communion, and partnership with the Lord and with one another. The absence of abiding in Christ, both individually and corporately, makes us lifeless, fruitless, and powerless.

Jesus said, "I am the vine, you are the branches. He who abides in Me, and I in him, bears much fruit; for without Me you can do nothing. If anyone does not abide in Me, he is cast out as a branch and is withered; and they gather them and throw them into the fire, and they are burned. If you abide in Me, and My words abide in you, you will ask what you desire, and it shall be done for you" (John 15:5–7).

Scofield put it this way:

> To abide in Christ is, on the one hand, to have no known sin unjudged and unconfessed, no interest into which He is not brought, no life which He cannot share. On the other hand, the abiding one takes all burdens to Him, and draws all wisdom, life, and strength from Him.[1]

Just as married couples belong to each other, reside together, and share one another's life and love, so too Christ and His bride, the church, must dwell together in intimate love, sharing one another's life.

The present impotent state of the church in North America is due to the widespread failure to abide in Christ in intimate love and communion. The church is not pursuing in prayer the intimate love relationship that is offered by Jesus' *gracious* presence. Therefore, many Christians never go on to seek His glorious presence.

## The Glorious Presence of Christ

Moses faced the heartbreaking experience of watching the Hebrew people worship before the golden calf. He poured out his heart to God, pleading, "Please, show me Your glory" (Exod. 33:18). Clearly, Moses needed this refreshing and encouraging experience. By asking to see the glory of God, he meant the Lord's majestic sovereignty, supreme power, and moral perfection.

Moses needed this fresh reminder that God is able to save His people. Moses also needed to see that God is not only able to save His people, but also He is gracious and full of compassion (v. 19). His power is *able* to save and His love is *abundant* to save, no matter what the cost.

Knowing the glorious presence of God is just as essential for our spiritual health and progress today as it was in the Old Testament. God's glorious presence has been manifested many times, not just in the church but also in the world down through the centuries.

After the tabernacle had been built according to God's specifications, His glorious presence filled the sanctuary (Exod. 40:34). The Lord's glory was so prevalent that Moses was not able to enter the tabernacle (v. 35). The majestic cloud remained over the sanctuary and later over the temple until it finally departed before the destruction of the latter, prior to the Babylonian captivity (Ezek. 10:18–22). After this, the majestic cloud did not return.

Isaiah also saw the glorious presence of God enthroned in the temple. This produced in Isaiah an overwhelming conviction of sin and revealed his need for moral and spiritual cleansing. God graciously cleansed him and commissioned him for service (Isa. 6).

Job saw the glorious presence of God at the close of his long period of suffering. He, too, was convicted of sin and repented (Job 42:1–6). Job then prayed for his misguided friends who had added to his affliction with their erroneous moral judgments (vv. 7–9). God restored to him twice as much as he had before (v. 10). The entire congregation of Israel saw God in all His glory when

He rebuked and destroyed Korah and the rebels who had slandered Him, Moses, and Aaron (Numbers 16).

Peter, James, and John saw Christ revealed in His glory on the Mount of Transfiguration (Matt. 17:1–8). John later wrote, "And the Word became flesh and dwelt among us, and we beheld His glory, the glory as of the only begotten of the Father, full of grace and truth" (John 1:14). The book of Revelation begins with a vision of Christ in all His glory (1:10–20). The Gospels usually portray Christ in His humility, namely, being despised and rejected, and we tend to think of Christ as a lamb. But our faith will remain weak until we recognize His great power and glory.

The glory of Christ permeates the book of Acts. There He appears as the mighty conqueror leading His church to crash the gates of hell and liberate Satan's captives from idolatry on a massive scale (16:18; 19:14–27).

God has displayed His glory in the church through great revivals such as the one that swept through Wales in 1904 and 1905. Christians were overwhelmed with a fresh realization of the greatness and majesty of God. They forsook sin and were drawn to spend hours, even whole nights, in prayer and singing praises to God. Instead of worshiping on the run, eager to get out of the morning church service, they took time to listen to God. They faced up to their sins, which had been forgotten, and made these matters right. For once in their life, they enjoyed God so much that they lingered in His presence for hours.

Events were canceled because so many folks preferred church over political rallies and sports. God's people discovered Him as their "exceeding joy" (Ps. 43:4). God's glorious presence in the church resulted in a "mighty, holy cleansing," and the whole country looked on in awe and wonder. Feuding churches found reconciliation. Christians, convicted of their heartless treatment of elderly parents, went to the poor house and brought their parents home with them.

God's glory displayed in the church made a powerful impact on society. Judges found themselves with no cases to try! The police, with time on their hands, formed quartets to sing in churches. Taverns emptied, their customers being caught up in the powerful movement of God in the land. The ponies that were used to pull the coal carts out of the mines were confused, for they couldn't understand the miner's commands, which had been purged of profanity!

Should we pray for God to show His glorious presence in the church today? Certainly! Just use Paul's prayer as a model. His petition in Ephesians 3:14–21 leads us step-by-step along a path that reaches its peak with the heart cry "to Him be glory in the church by Christ Jesus to all generations, forever and ever. Amen." (Though we talk about it elsewhere, it serves us well to focus on Paul's prayer here.)

First, Paul asked that we would be strengthened by the vast unlimited power of the Spirit (v. 16), making Christ completely at home in our hearts by faith (v. 17). Next, the apostle prayed that we would become rooted and grounded in the love of Christ so that we would know by experience the Savior's love, which surpasses knowledge (vv. 17–19). Then Paul prayed that the church would be filled with all the fullness of God! At this point, the Lord's glorious presence completely dominates the church, displaying His supreme power and beautiful moral perfection.

Did Paul actually think that this *could* and *would* happen? Obviously, he did. Verse 20 says, "Now to Him who is able to do exceedingly abundantly above all that we ask or think, according to the power that works in us." God can certainly do this. Paul's prayer closes with God's glory displayed in the church "to all generations, forever and ever. Amen" (v. 21).

Our generation has not seen God's glory displayed in the church as it was in 1904–1905. Consequently, we have neglected this prayer and thus have lowered our spiritual vision. We forget that God's standard is *His glory*. "For all have sinned and fall short of the glory of God" (Rom. 3:23). The human race faces ruination as a result.

We ought not to be duped! Falling short of God's glory is *not* acceptable in the eyes of the Lord. We have been chosen for the praise of God's glory (Eph. 1:12, 14). In chapter 3, Paul called on us to pray that we might actually see God's glory fully displayed in His church. Christians can and should glorify God in their bodies and in their spirits (1 Cor. 6:20). "Therefore, whether you eat or drink, or whatever you do, do all to the glory of God" (10:31).

We suffer a great loss from aiming too low. We're like the car rental company that boasted, "We're No. 2," which meant, "We don't try." Obviously with human effort alone we cannot live to the praise of God's glory as individuals, as families, and as churches. This only comes about through the almighty working of God in our hearts. It underscores all the more that we need to pray biblical petitions, such as the one Paul uttered! Then we should trust God to perform things that are above and beyond our own abilities.

United prayer for the fulfillment of the high calling of God in the church has reached the point of paramount importance. The church can only fulfill its calling though constant dependence on God to fulfill His purpose in us. By faith, we can attain this high calling.

## Review Questions

1. Name the three critical aspects of Christ's presence.
2. What happened as the psalmist meditated on the God of compassion and love?
3. What was the psalmist's motivation for wanting to defend God's honor?
4. People who run away from God need to understand what two truths?
5. The psalmist asked God to lead him "in the way everlasting." What does this mean?
6. What would happen if married couples, families, small fellowship groups, and even entire congregations waited on God in prayer until the joy, hope, and holiness of Christ's presence was fully realized?

7. The analogy of the church (the bride of Christ) and Christ (the suitor) is given to make what contrast?
8. What is one of the great purposes of prayer and Bible study?
9. Of all Jesus' followers, who understood that He was about to die?
10. According to Deuteronomy 34:10, how well did God know Moses?
11. According to Psalm 27:8, what does the Lord desire of His followers?
12. How did Jesus know who His friends were?
13. What harm can come from "little" sins?
14. What would you say is the cause of the present impotent state of the church in North America? Why?
    a. too much money, affluence, and luxuries
    b. failure to abide in Christ in intimate love and communion
    c. lack of prayer
15. When Moses knew the Hebrew people had worshiped before the golden calf, what did he pray?
16. We tend to think of Christ only as a lamb. But our faith will remain weak until we see:
    a. revival in the church?
    b. giving to the church increase?
    c. God's great power and glory?
    d. more prayer?
17. How should we petition God to show His glorious presence in the church today?
18. Why has our generation not seen God's glory displayed in the church?
    a. We have neglected prayer.
    b. We have lowered our vision.
    c. We have forgotten that God's standard is *His glory.*
    d. all of the above
19. Have you ever implored God to make His residence in your home or church?

20. What would you expect a church or home to be like if Christ was a permanent resident?
21. In what ways is Christ the leader of your congregation? In what ways is He not?
22. If you knew that Christ would lead your home, what would you ask Him to change?

*Exercises*

1. Pray with the rest of your family and collectively ask Christ to take charge of your home.
2. Pray with another member of your church for Christ to become a permanent resident of your congregation.

# SECOND KEY:
## THE POWER AND REAL MEANING OF PRAYING IN JESUS' NAME

*Therefore God also has highly exalted Him and given Him the name which is above every name, that at the name of Jesus every knee should bow, of those in heaven, and of those on earth, and of those under the earth, and that every tongue should confess that Jesus Christ is Lord, to the glory of God the Father. (Phil. 2:9–11)*

## CHAPTER FIVE

# Discovering the Power and Real Meaning of Praying in Jesus' Name

THE SECOND KEY FOR effective prayer with Christ in charge is to pray in the power of Jesus' name. Many Christians, however, do not understand what it really means to pray in His name.

I was teaching a seminar on prayer when someone asked, "What did Jesus mean when He promised to answer prayers offered in His name?" This person was referring to Jesus' promise in John 14:13–14, which states, "And whatever you ask in My name, that I will do, that the Father may be glorified in the Son. If you ask anything in My name, I will do it" (see also 15:16 and 16:23–26).

Consider the magnitude of this promise! There are some prayer promises that may be answered with a "yes," "no," or "wait," but not this one. Jesus said, "And whatever you ask in My name, that I will do." The possibilities are vast, stretching far beyond our natural limitations. This is a "God-sized" promise.

The Bible makes it clear that there is no need God cannot meet. "And my God shall supply all your need according to His riches in glory by Christ Jesus" (Phil. 4:19). We find a special word of encouragement through God's promise to the fainthearted. "I can do all things through Christ who strengthens me" (v. 13). Second Corinthians 9:8 is a broad promise that says, "And God is able to make all grace abound toward you, that you, always having all sufficiency in all things, may have an abundance for every good work."

As we absorb the promises, instructions, commandments, and prayers of Scripture, we discover something to our utter amazement! God is searching for opportunities to show Himself strong on our behalf (2 Chron. 16:9).

Pause and dwell on the following truths for a moment. We can see that God not only is interested in patching up our tattered lives, but He also is interested in teaching us to live far above our fallen world, enabling us to experience a new dimension of truth with power and zeal. He wants us to enjoy the fullness of our new life in the Kingdom of Light, the Kingdom of Life, and the Kingdom of God. In right relationship with God, we can confidently ask our Lord to turn the impossible into the possible. This is God's specialty. "For with God nothing will be impossible" (Luke 1:37).

Jesus challenged His disciples to ask for the impossible and believe that it would be done.

> Have faith in God. For assuredly, I say to you, whoever says to this mountain, "Be removed and be cast into the sea," and does not doubt in his heart, but believes that those things he says will be done, he will have whatever he says. Therefore I say to you, whatever things you ask when you pray, believe that you receive them, and you will have them. (Mark 11:22–24)

God urged Jeremiah to ask Him for things far above the prophet's limited knowledge or experience. "Call to Me, and I will answer you, and show you great and mighty things, which you do not know" (Jer. 33:3; see also 32:17, 27.) Paul exuberantly closed one of his prayers in words far surpassing mere positive thinking. "Now to Him who is able to do exceedingly abundantly above all that we ask or think, according to the power that works in us, to Him be glory in the church by Christ Jesus to all generations, forever and ever. Amen" (Eph. 3:20–21).

Upon our new birth and conversion to the Lord Jesus Christ,

we receive His supernatural life. Living in the power of Christ is absolutely essential for being spiritually victorious. It is up to us *to claim* Jesus' life and power. His life makes us a new people who are empowered with a convincing message to all humankind.

## Misconceptions About Praying in Jesus' Name

The words "in Jesus' name" have become a trite phrase commonly used to close prayers, but the *power* of Jesus' name is generally missing. What a tragic loss! All power in heaven and earth is unleashed when we truly pray in Jesus' name. What did Jesus really mean when He made this promise? We may begin our search for the answer to this question by taking a look at some of the misconceptions about praying "in Jesus' name."

Jesus was not promising that we will get what we want by merely closing our prayers in His name. In fact, none of the prayers in the New Testament close with the phrase "in Jesus' name." For example, notice Paul's prayers in Ephesians 1:15–23; 3:14–21; Philippians 1:9; Colossians 1:9–14; and 1 Thessalonians 3:11–13. If Jesus intended for our prayers to close with the phrase "in Jesus' name," surely Paul's petitions would have used those words. But they did not.

Is it *wrong* to close our prayers by saying "in Jesus' name?" No! After all, people were baptized "in the name of Jesus Christ" (Acts 2:38). The lame man was healed "in the name of Jesus Christ of Nazareth" (3:6). The apostles proclaimed salvation through faith in His name (4:12).

The problem lies in the realization that ending prayers "in Jesus' name" has become an empty formality that is devoid of meaning and power for most Christians today. Sincere believers close their prayers by saying "in Jesus' name" without the slightest assurance that they will receive their requests. Worse still, anyone can say the words "in Jesus' name" as a sort of magic formula without even belonging to Christ!

In Acts 19:13–17, some Jewish exorcists who did not know or serve the Lord Jesus Christ attempted to cast out evil spirits by invoking His name. But their plan backfired. One evil spirit even replied, "Jesus I know, and Paul I know; but who are you?" Then the person possessed by the demon leaped on these men and beat them up. They subsequently fled out of the house naked and wounded.

Praying in the name of Jesus can be a fraudulent act, like forging a name on a stolen check. Strangely enough, the inappropriate use of Jesus' name may be attended by great and mighty works. Many have been deceived by this.

One of the most disturbing indictments in the New Testament shows Christ condemning false followers. These false followers had convinced themselves of their "genuine" standing before God because of the mighty works they performed in Jesus' name. Christ said, "Many will say to Me in that day, 'Lord, Lord, have we not prophesied in Your name, cast out demons in Your name, and done many wonders in Your name?' And then I will declare to them, 'I never knew you; depart from Me, you who practice lawlessness!'" (Matt. 7:22–23).

The false followers had never taken refuge under the lordship of Christ. They claimed to serve Jesus, but in reality, they devoted themselves to living according to their own will. They blatantly used the name of Jesus to exalt themselves.

If this isn't bad enough, it gets worse. These lawless ones actually prepare the way for the false Christ, who is known as "the lawless one." Paul warned, "The coming of the lawless one is according to the working of Satan, with all power, signs, and lying wonders" (2 Thess. 2:9). Apparently *many* will be caught up in this terrible error and deception. Mighty works alone do not prove that miracle workers are bound for heaven. They may be on their way to hell. *So who does have the right to pray in Jesus' name?*

## Rightly Praying in Jesus' Name

In order to pray in Jesus' name, the first order of business is to become a child of God by believing on the Lord Jesus Christ (John

1:12; 2:23; 3:18; 14:6; Acts 4:12; 1 John 5:13). You must believe that there is no one else who can save you from sin. Believing includes repentance in which you turn to the only living and true God from idols (1 Thess. 1:9). Popular "idols" in America are people and things that are used to fill the void where God is supposed to reign. The most popular idol of our day is *self*.

By believing in Christ, you awaken to the knowledge of the true God. You also begin to worship and serve Him, especially while you wait for the return of His Son from heaven (1 Thess. 1:9–10). This is what faith and repentance are all about. As children of God, we then commit ourselves to live under His authority by being baptized in His name. In Matthew 28:18–20, we are taught to baptize new believers in the name of the Father, Son, and Holy Spirit, and to teach them to obey the Lord Jesus Christ. The name we use in this instance is not a rigid formula (note the variations in Acts 2:38 and 8:16).

The power is not in some exactly stated formula. Rather, the power is in the person of the Lord Jesus Christ, through whom we are related to the Father by means of the Holy Spirit. The secret power of praying in Jesus' name is related to our faith in Christ and our loving obedience to Him (Matt. 28:20).

We are truly asking in Jesus' name when we operate under God's authority as His representatives. Jesus marveled at the great faith of the centurion who believed that He could speak with all the power of God to heal his servant. The centurion declared, "For I *also* am a man under authority" (8:9; emphasis added). This Roman army officer perceived that Jesus lived under the authority of God, just as the centurion himself served under the power of Caesar.

This representative of the emperor possessed amazing insight. Jesus came in His Father's name, and thus Christ was under God's authority (John 5:43). He did nothing from His own initiative but always did the Father's will (5:19, 30; 12:49–50). Jesus was the perfect representative of God. He authoritatively claimed, "He who has seen Me has seen the Father" (14:9). Therefore, Jesus acted in the power and authority of the Father.

We have been sent into the world to represent, not ourselves, but Christ (John 20:21). All authority and power in heaven and earth has been given to the Lord Jesus Christ to empower us in fulfilling His commission to us (Matt. 28:18–20; Acts 1:8). We can pray with power in His name when we faithfully live under His authority as His representatives. "And whatever you do in word or deed, do all in the name of the Lord Jesus, giving thanks to the Father through Him" (Col. 3:17). *But how do we prepare ourselves to pray for that which is humanly impossible, fully confident that God will answer our prayers?*

## The Real Objective: Glorifying the Father in the Son

Once again, Jesus gives us the answer. "And whatever you ask in My name, that I will do, *that the Father may be glorified in the Son*" (John 14:13; emphasis added). Children of God may receive many answers to prayer without ever fully understanding the meaning of praying in Jesus' name. However, many strive in vain to pray in the power of Jesus' name, all the while hoping that their desperate needs will be met. Tragically they receive no answer.

These believers may be burdened over family members in bondage to evil. They may be praying to overcome some habitual sins in their own lives. Perhaps they are in bitter conflict with their spouse or children, or someone at church or at their job. They pray about these matters but receive no answers.

Why can't these people claim the promise found in John 14:13–14? We must pause here and point out that there are mysteries involved in unanswered prayers. Praying in Jesus' name requires gaining the assurance that our prayers are completely in harmony with His sovereign will. There is also the need to learn to wait for God's time. And as we pray, we need to be humble before the Lord.

Before George Mueller committed himself to persevere in prayer for something, he would first seek confirmation that his request was in the sovereign will of God. When he gained that assurance, he prayed persistently, sometimes for many years, until he received what he asked for.

Certainly nothing is amiss from God's perspective. He still specializes in the impossible, doesn't He! The impossible still brings great glory to God, doesn't it! He gave Abraham and Sarah a child in their old age. He parted the Red Sea so that Israel could escape the onslaught of Pharaoh's army. The Lord defeated a huge army arrayed against Israel, using Gideon's little group of three hundred soldiers. Jesus fed the five thousand by multiplying a child's lunch. He gave the disciples a miraculous catch of fish. Christ transformed the apostles from cowards to bold witnesses who were completely willing to risk their lives for Him.

We don't know all the reasons for unanswered prayers. However, we do know that one reason prayers are not answered is because we tend to ask for selfish reasons. "You ask and do not receive, because you ask amiss, that you may spend it on your pleasures" (James 4:3).

A pastor may pray for the salvation of the lost and for growing attendance in his church. Is this bad? It may be, especially if he is trying to make himself look good to beef up his résumé so that he can get hired by a larger church.

Some women asked a minister to pray for their husbands to get saved and delivered from their addiction to alcohol. The minister wisely asked, "Why do you want them to be delivered? Is it just because their drunkenness causes you so much trouble? What if God delivers your husbands and then wants to use them in His service? Would you be willing for them to serve the Lord, no matter what it costs you?" In due course, the wives were willing, and their husbands were saved and used by God.

On one occasion I met a man who had overcome alcohol addiction through his own efforts. He was so proud of this achievement that he claimed, "I don't need to go to church!" He was further from God than when he was addicted!

One of my daughters asked me, "Dad, would you pray for God to give me a husband?" "I will, if you will tell the Lord that if He wants you to be single, you will accept it and learn to be happy without a husband." She burst into tears before she replied, "I will, but it will be hard." God did give her a wonderful husband, but only after she left the choice of being single or married with Him.

The choice ultimately is God's to make. Prayers must be offered in such a way as to bring ultimate glory to Him. In prayer, we must honor the Father as the supreme ruler of the universe and of us.

This principle sums up the prayers and the life of Paul. From prison, the apostle wrote that some of his fellow Christians preached Christ "from selfish ambition, not sincerely, supposing to add affliction to my chains" (Phil. 1:16). How did Paul respond? He remarked, "that in every way, whether in pretense or in truth, Christ is preached; and in this I rejoice, yes, and will rejoice" (v. 18). Paul's one desire was for Christ to be magnified, whether through his life or death (v. 20).

We can ask anything in Jesus' name—even the impossible—and expect to receive it, but only if we are living in complete subjection to Him and if our sole motive is to magnify, glorify, and honor Christ alone. *What prevents this type of praying today?*

## The Power to Lock and Unlock the Heavens

In reality, God's people backslide. In disobedience, we lose the power and authority of God's name. God hasn't lost His authority, but by our sinning we drift away from His authority over us. Prayer loses power and eventually becomes a dead formality. This calamity is not unique to our time. It permeated Israel in Elijah's day. God's people began to worship an idol named Baal. Elijah was passionately jealous for God's reputation and glory as the sovereign Lord of Israel. The prophet prayed that it might not rain in order to bring God's temporal judgment on the land until the people were broken of worshiping a false god and returned to the Lord in repentance and faith.

Elijah strode into the presence of wicked King Ahab and boldly announced, "As the LORD God of Israel lives, before whom I stand, there shall not be dew nor rain these years, except at my word" (1 Kings 17:1). The prophet's confidence in God's authority over rain and drought gave him unquenchable boldness before people. He was completely submissive to God. Elijah prayed according to the dictates of God's Word. The prophet's motivation was based solely upon his overwhelming desire to see the Lord honored in Israel as the only true and living God (Deut. 11:16–17). So Elijah confidently claimed the power and authority of God's name.

Three and a half years later, Israel was desperate for rain. The drought had run its course. Again, Elijah appeared before the king. This time the prophet admonished Ahab to summon the four hundred fifty prophets of Baal, whom Elijah was challenging in a contest. The intent was to see which deity could answer the request for fire to come down from heaven and burn up a sacrifice.

The prophets of Baal built an altar and begged their lifeless and powerless idol to send fire to consume the bull that they had prepared for sacrifice. All day, they desperately cried in vain to their idol until the time came for the evening sacrifice. Finally it was Elijah's turn. He ordered that his sacrifice be soaked with water to make the impending miracle all the more obvious. He then prayed, and God powerfully answered his request.

> Lord God of Abraham, Isaac, and Israel, let it be known this day that you are God in Israel and I am Your servant, and that I have done all these things at Your word. Hear me, O Lord, hear me, that this people may know that You are the Lord God, and that You have turned their hearts back to You again. Then the fire of the Lord fell and consumed the burnt sacrifice. (1 Kings 18:36–38)

Prayer offered in the power of God's name exposes the difference between lifeless idols and the true and living God. Furthermore, the Lord's answer identifies His loyal, obedient servants and validates their witness.

Our society today mocks Christians and our message by saying, "We don't believe your God is the only supreme Ruler. We reject you and your arrogant ways, especially your claim to be His representatives." Their criticism of us is partly justified. Elijah prayed for God to restore backslidden Israel. Today, we need to pray for the restoration of backslidden Christians.

In the New Testament, God reminds us that we should fervently and patiently pray like Elijah to restore those who wander away from the truth (James 5:16–20). We desperately need the fire of God in our hearts and in our pulpits. The watching world needs a fresh demonstration that God still lives. The people of God need fresh proof of the power of praying in Jesus' name.

Remarkably, God gives us refreshing experiences of His power by answering our prayers with heaven's fire. A friend of Bible Prayer Fellowship sent me a news clipping regarding a powerful, holy cleansing of the students in a Christian school in Peoria, Illinois. Broken relationships were healed. The lost were saved. I knew that such a transforming work of the Spirit could only happen where a group had truly prayed in Jesus' name. Truly invoking Jesus' name in prayer always brings Him into the midst of His people to actively take charge. Life-transforming blessings can only come from our Lord.

Let's rejoice together as we look at what happened in Peoria in answer to prayer. However, as we do so we must bear in mind that genuine praying in Jesus' name does not always bring the more tangible blessings we crave. In some cases, prayer in Jesus' name may bring His comforting presence, which enables a child of God to endure rejection or even persecution with much grace (Acts 5:41; 7:59–60).

## When the Fire Fell in Peoria

A most remarkable fire followed a basketball game on Friday, February 7, 1997, in Peoria, Illinois. Students from Peoria Christian School (PCS) gathered around a bonfire to praise God, while they tossed into the fire "anything that hinders my walk with the Lord." Tossed items included satanic magic and sorcery books, cigarettes, cocaine, marijuana, heroin, CDs with anti-Christian music, pornographic videos, books, and magazines. They also poured liquor and beer on the ground.

One boy threw $3,000 worth of CDs into the fire. Another kid peeled a shirt off his back with the name and number of a certain player for the Pittsburg Steelers. The student confessed that this player had been his idol. A wealthy boy threw money in the fire because it had been his idol. An eighteen-year-old senior from East Peoria said, "God has set me free from drugs, alcohol, and cigarettes."

A photographer from the *Journal Star* newspaper took hundreds of pictures. The picture they published showed a boy towering above the crowd with his face lifted up to heaven. He was not that tall, but the photographer caught him in midair as he leaped for joy over his new-found faith in Christ.

Prior to this life-changing week, the teachers had complained that this was the worst senior class in the forty-year history of the school. Now they say it was the best senior class ever.

The seniors had been bitterly divided over how to use the $11,000 they had saved for their senior trip. During the special meetings led by Tom Mahairas from Manhattan Bible Church, the seniors had been reconciled to one another. When they heard that Manhattan Bible Church's drug rehabilitation program needed $12,000, the seniors unanimously agreed to donate their $11,000.

When news of the seniors' gift got out, monetary gifts began pouring in for their trip. On May 17, they went to New York City for a senior trip that was devoted to witnessing under the leadership of Manhattan Bible Church.

The senior's reconciliation earlier in the week led the way to a Friday session that swept through the student body of four hundred fifty. Tom Mahairas challenged the students who were gathered in the gym to get out of their comfort zone and take their stand in the commitment zone.

Nearly all of the students poured out of the bleachers onto

the floor of the gym, where they engaged in repentance, confession, reconciliation, and conversation. One girl rushed to ask forgiveness of another girl with such speed that she almost tackled her.

Pastor Wilson Green of Peoria's Fellowship Bible Church said that about thirty ministers had been praying for revival in Peoria for five years. Green, who is a member of the PCS board, said that a turning point at PCS took place in 1996 when twelve students and their adult sponsors went to Vladimir, Russia, in an exchange program that had gone on for several years. In 1996, the students were frustrated because they were getting nowhere in their witness. They seemed to face deadness. So they were praying for a breakthrough.

The boys and men were praying late into the night when they were humbled and brought to their knees under the mighty power of God. Around midnight, they decided to go to the girls' quarters to tell them about this unusual moving of God in their prayers. The girls praised the Lord because they had been praying that the boys would get over being lukewarm!

When this group returned to PCS, they continued to meet several mornings a week, praying for the school and the student body. Other students joined them in prayer. Finally, they asked permission to have a lock-in so that they could spend a night in prayer and praise. Over seventy students took part.

A growing movement of student prayer continued until the powerful moving of God during the February meetings. The students chose as the theme of those meetings, "Get real! How to live your faith in the world." This theme gives definition and direction to the students now that the excitement of the special meetings is over.

Teams of students are going out to other schools, youth groups, and churches to share what God has done in their lives and to issue their call to "Get real!" God is awakening many young people and adults to take possession of new life in Christ. Many Bible study groups have started among the PCS students.

We had a group of these students come to our church in

Dallas, Texas, and share their testimony of how God changed their lives and their school in answer to prayer. The congregation prayed for God's movement among young people in the city. About four hundred fifty young people with their sponsors gathered for a rally with these students from Peoria on a hot Monday night in July. The student team gave testimony of God's gracious work in changing their lives. A most gracious work of God followed.

There were eighteen confessions of faith in Christ reported, and groups of students met with their sponsors afterward. Some were weeping as they got right with God and one another. Some groups continued in prayer and spiritual renewal until 2 A.M. We had experienced the power of prayer in Jesus' name. He was quite obviously present and actively blessing us all!

## Review Questions

1. According to John 14:13–14, does God answer our prayers "in Jesus name" with either "yes," "no," or "wait"?
2. If God is not only interested in putting ointment on our skinned shins and patching up our tattered lives, then what else is He interested in?
3. Jesus challenged His disciples to ask for the impossible. What ingredient makes this possible?
4. What was Jeremiah's concept of prayer?
5. How did Paul view prayer?
6. How many prayers in the New Testament end with the phrase "in Jesus' name?"
7. What did Jesus say to false followers who claimed that they had done mighty works in His name?
8. Does Satan have the authority to duplicate God's miraculous power? Give the chapter and verse from 2 Thessalonians.
9. What are the ingredients for the power of praying in Jesus' name?
10. What is the *real* objective of praying in Jesus' name?
    a. for God to prove Himself to us

   b. to get our prayers answered

   c. to glorify the Father in the Son

   d. to change us

 11. Why does God want us to ask for the impossible?

 12. Give three scriptural examples of God's mighty, miraculous intervention.

 13. Name one reason why God refuses to answer some of our prayers:

   a. God is too busy.

   b. God is too weak.

   c. Our motives are not pure.

   d. We didn't end the prayer with the phrase "in Jesus' name."

 14. What should be our sole motive in prayer?

 15. What gave Elijah unquenchable boldness before people?

   a. Elijah was taller than most.

   b. Elijah had confidence in God's authority to do what He promised.

   c. Elijah had excellent communication skills.

 16. When Elijah asked God to send down fire from heaven, what was the intention of his prayer?

   a. to make fools out of the prophets of Baal

   b. to prove that the Lord of Israel alone was God

   c. to emphasize Elijah's authority as a prophet

 17. What is your primary objective when praying for personal needs? For church needs?

 18. Share an example of when God answered your prayer in a mighty way. What was the object of the request?

 19. Do you think Christ wants to answer our prayers?

 20. Do you feel there is power in your prayers?

*Exercises*

 1. Write down five prayers for your home, small group, or church. Confirm the motive behind each prayer and, if appropriate, ask God to answer the request, being confident of the power of Christ to bring it about.

2. Pray that your marrige partner or small group will share the study of this book with you and unite in practicing praying with Christ obviously present and actively in charge, changing each one as He sees fit, and leading you to pray in harmony with the Father's will.

# THIRD KEY:
## ASKING CHRIST TO TAKE CHARGE

*Worthy is the Lamb who was slain to receive power and riches and wisdom, and strength and honor and glory and blessing! (Rev. 5:12)*

## CHAPTER SIX

# The Power of Christ's Active Leadership: Lost and Found

In the book of Acts, we saw a powerful church full of heavenly love and holiness. Today, Christian homes and churches of this caliber seem to be the rare exception, not the rule. Within the church, we see intense power struggles, even fights. In Christian families, broken marriages are all too common. Even in lives where no blatant sin exists, there is noticeable spiritual dullness. Serious problems of spiritual weakness plague the church. Instead of the gospel turning the world upside down, the world is turning the church upside down, inside out, and every way but loose! The sins of the world have become the sins of the church.

Our Lord promised to fill families and churches with His presence and His own holy life through the power of the Holy Spirit. But what has happened? Something is missing! In this chapter we will discover the most common reason why Christ is not actively in charge of so many churches today.

Even ministers are not immune. The newspapers go into a feeding frenzy over a minister who allegedly attempted to murder his wife, a cleric who was involved in adulterous affairs for decades, and priests who are accused of being pedophiles.

"Just when we thought the world was again becoming safe for preaching, headlines burned with a sad and startling story of a fallen brother," writes Joseph Stowell, president of Moody Bible Institute. He confides, "I find myself asking, 'Is there something within our system that tends to produce neatly packaged products looking for a place to fall?'"[1]

Can you see it? Joseph Stowell has let loose an arrow that is right on target! There indeed is "something within our system that tends to produce neatly packaged products looking for a place to fall." I'm talking about a hidden fault lurking beneath the surface. It weakens our resistance, not only to the lure of lust but also to all kinds of temptations. More importantly, it destroys our pursuit of Christlikeness. It leaves churches and their members cut off from the direction and power of Christ (our Head), not to mention one another. Except for our religious veneer, the church often bears a remarkable resemblance to our decadent American culture.

This hidden fault has not made the headlines as a scandal. Instead of dealing with this fault, we cover it up or disguise it in various forms. We even turn it into a matter of respectability in the best of churches. You will find religious people hotly defending this deadly spiritual virus. We have come to justify or rationalize anything and everything. Some defend this virus as a form of liberty, while others fight back in the harsh, legalistic tradition of the self-righteous Pharisees. These opposing forces have their source in the same underlying fault.

And what is this deadly fault? Is it materialism? Immorality? Have we undermined the reliability of Scripture? Have we turned the church into a big business? Just what is this fault?

A Gallup poll makes it abundantly clear what this fault is. Gallup even put a label on it. They call it "a self-centered kind of faith." Whereas, preaching on hell and the coming judgment of God is rare, private religion is "in"! The church seems to exist to lead people to self-fulfillment, that is, to feel good about themselves. We have lost the perspective of the awesome holiness of God. We falter in our zeal to see the consuming glory of God manifested in our lives, families, churches, communities, and country. This "self-centered kind of faith" has its roots in pagan America, not in the Bible.

As a nation, we have become a people resounding with the words, "everyone did that which is right in his own eyes" (Judg. 17:6; 21:25). We major in self-centeredness and self-gratification, while we minor in self-control and self-restraint. We have adopted a view of liberty that produces chaos. It breeds our own destruction.

A motorist was arrested in San Diego some years ago for driving while intoxicated. In court, he argued that he had a constitutional right to drive in this condition. He was, after all, engaged in the "pursuit of happiness."

Justice William O. Douglas wrote *Points of Rebellion* while he was still on the Supreme Court in 1969. In it he said, "It's wonderful to be back in a nation where even a riot may be tolerated."[2] In the same book he wrote, "But where grievances pile high and most of the elected spokesmen represent the Establishment, violence may be the only effective response."[3] Appropriately, portions of the book were originally published in Playboy, the champion of hedonism, situation ethics, and the destroyer of moral absolutes.

This kind of warped logic spills over into the church, especially when a major conflict ensues. The church itself faces a crisis of credibility when members actively rebel or passively ignore major tenets of Christianity. One pastor observed, "Many people are tired of church organization. They are prone to say, 'You don't have to be baptized; you don't need to become a member. So why bother with church organizations and formalities?'"

This "self-centered kind of faith" is not limited to people who want only a loose connection with the local church. Many active members who attend regularly refuse to bring themselves into accountability with the church. Worse still, they refuse to line up with the clear teaching of Scripture or submit to Christ in obedience to His Headship. Some even go so far as to bring lawsuits against the church.

These lawsuits sometimes arise over church discipline. People have joined the church without ever being told that baptized members are expected to commit themselves to be disciples who are learning to obey all that Christ commanded (Matt. 28:18–20). This baptismal commitment becomes the basis for holding members accountable for their conduct (18:15–20).

Without this kind of commitment, many people sit in churches today thinking that their behavior is strictly their own private business. One man who admitted having an adulterous affair bluntly told his pastor (who came to call him to repentance), "I tend to my business and you should tend to yours." Some of the members of a Bible-believing church agreed with that!

How can Christ be honored as head of a church where obedience to Him is entirely up to each individual? There is no corporate commitment to Him! You can join nearly any church in America, liberal or conservative, without ever making a commitment to learn to live by biblical standards. You can even become a leader without ever becoming accountable or agreeing to obey all that Christ commanded (Matt. 28:18–20). Dallas Willard commented on this subject:

> And the current position of the church in our world may be better explained by what liberals and conservatives have shared, rather than by how they differ. For it is for different reasons, and with different emphases, that they have agreed that discipleship to Christ is optional to membership in the Christian church. Thus, the very type of life that could change the course of human society and upon occasion has done so is excluded from the essential message of the church.[4]

As proof, Willard argues that:

> The best of current literature on discipleship either states outright or assumes that the Christian may not be a disciple at all—even after a lifetime as a church member."[5]

Worse still, many church members think that their participation in the local church is completely unrelated to their fellowship with Christ! In their fuzzy thinking, they believe that they can wholly follow the Lord while totally ignoring Him as the active head of the church they attend.

## Church Leaders Share the Blame

Sad to say, blame does not lie solely with the "lone rangers" who sit in the pews each Sunday morning. Many church officers attempt to lead without waiting on God and humbling themselves in prayer or adequately preparing their heart to deliver God's Word. Consequently, their authority is prone to be misused, and they get "off track." Often, this opens the door to "lawlessness." So many fights break out in the church that some people are afraid to commit themselves to any congregation.

A Bible conference teacher made a confession that struck me as being off base. He said, "My wife and I attend church, but we avoid getting involved." A lady had approached him seeking advice on how to cope with devastating strife in her church. He further explained, "My wife and I have gone through so much turmoil that we decided to refuse any added church responsibility. We just attend." I saw his comments as an indictment of both his church and himself.

This speaker clearly did not realize the serious implications of attending church as "lone rangers," rather than as members of the body of Christ. He failed to see the importance of gathering together with God's people under the active headship of Christ.

In reality, this kind of detached relationship is quite common. Whenever the subject of "commitment" comes up in pastors' meetings, those present unanimously lament the lack of it among their parishioners. Ed Dayton, in his book entitled *Whatever Happened to Commitment?*, sees this lack of commitment as a critical problem threatening to destroy our society, our homes, and our churches. He confessed that on one occasion he discovered a serious lack of commitment in his own life. This came to light when Ed accepted a job offer that required him to move far away from his church.

"Ed, we need you here," his pastor pled. "We won't be the same without you." Ed took it as a compliment and moved anyway. Later, he realized that he had been a vital link in that local body of Christ. He lamented, "It continued to hurt that church for years to come. I never asked my local fellowship what God was saying to them."[6]

Ed realized that Christian commitment starts as an individual matter, but that it can never end there. Being an individual is good and right, for we are born again on an individual basis. But the Holy Spirit assigns us to our place in the church, which is the living body of Christ. Our union with Christ and one another has made us part of a redeemed community of faith.

## The Deathknell of the Church

Making individualism and personal self-interest our primary commitment denies us the power and reality of our new relationship with Christ. It also makes our churches more at home with our fallen world than with Christ and His kingdom. The famous French author Alexis de Tocqueville wrote, "Individualism, at first, only saps the virtues of public life; but in the long run, it attacks and destroys all others; and is at length absorbed in downright selfishness."[7]

Making personal self-interest their primary commitment has produced a multitude of frustrated church members. They are bewildered because they are not experiencing the spiritually abundant life promised in the Gospels and demonstrated in Acts. Even worse, churches lose their heavenly character, direction, and power because many leaders and members believe that the Holy Spirit's power is no longer available today.

The all-powerful Holy Spirit is still here, earnestly desiring to reproduce Christ in individuals, small groups, families, and churches. However, He is hindered. His attempts to rekindle the fire of faith have been doused with the cold water of unbelief. In fact, He even encounters stubborn resistance. People are "uncomfortable" talking about the Holy Spirit. Therefore, the church falls short of the abundant life. Many Christians go through life stranded in the "no man's land" between the Kingdom of Light and the Kingdom of Darkness, the Kingdom of Life and the Kingdom of Death.

We dare not keep this up! We can't go on in this condition! The church must repent and return to Christ. We need earnestly to seek the Lord to find out how we have grieved the Spirit. Doing this will enable us to confess and forsake our sins and recover the abundant life for the Savior's glory. Otherwise, we will drift downhill to destruction under the judgment of God. Israel's history serves as a warning to us.

Our generation of Christians resembles the generation of Israel that escaped from Egypt. Frustrated and rebellious, they died in the desert because they refused to trust God to conquer their enemies. All the while, God wanted to bring them into the promised land, which was flowing with milk and honey in great abundance. Three times the New Testament warns the church against following the bad example of Israel's unbelieving wanderers. These examples show how unbelieving, self-centered Christianity slides downhill to destruction.

First, there is the warning to the carnal, self-centered Corinthian church, which was dominated by fights, immorality, and idolatry (1 Cor. 10:1–14). They looked just like sinful Israel in the desert. The Corinthians needed to wake up and flee from idolatry. Second, in Hebrews 3–4, Christians are warned against departing from the living God in unbelief, just as the generation of Israel did in the desert when they aborted their entrance into the promised land (Heb. 3:12).

Third, in Jude, we see the ultimate ruin of unbelieving, self-centered Christianity. False teachers sneak into the church and distort the grace of God. They give approval to outrageous sin and boldly deny the lordship of the Father and Son (v. 4). These evil teachers "reject authority" (v. 8). Such distorted Christianity faces destruction, just as did the unbelieving generation of Israel, the fallen angels, and the debased cities of Sodom and Gomorrah (vv. 5–7).

## The Starting Point of Change

What must we do to escape this deadly, self-centered form of Christianity? What will it take to become a spiritually pure and powerful church, one that is full of Christ and His love? What does God require for us to become more like the church in the book of Acts?

We must wake up and face the truth! We have forsaken our first love, namely, Christ (Rev. 2:4). We have become halfhearted in our obedience to Him. We are lukewarm. Christ admonishes, "I know your works, that you are neither cold nor hot. I could wish you were cold or hot. So then, because you are lukewarm, and neither cold nor hot, I will vomit you out of My mouth" (3:15–16).

We must repent and become passionately zealous to love, honor, and obey the Lord no matter how great the cost (v. 19). We must become like the church in Acts. When faced with an official demand to stop witnessing in His name, the early believers demonstrated their ardent devotion and obedience to Christ by praying in one accord. Instead of asking for help to escape persecution, they prayed for boldness and power to keep right on witnessing (Acts 4:23–35). They wanted to be true to Christ no matter what the cost! When the apostles—now ablaze with Holy Spirit power—were beaten for their loyalty to Christ, they rejoiced that they were counted worthy to suffer shame on His behalf (5:41).

Churches must return to Christ. We need a return to the passion and commitment of our "first love." When we do, we will see "a mighty, holy cleansing." Many broken lives will be mended overnight. Life-transforming power will be restored. The church will once again speak with convincing moral authority to our pagan society, and multitudes in the watching world will be inexplicably drawn to the Savior.

## A Practical Example

This is what happened at Ebenezer Baptist Church in Saskatoon, Saskatchewan, Canada, in 1971. It came about after the members of the congregation devoted themselves to prayer for almost two years.

Searching for the power of Christ to transform his flock, Pastor Bill McLeod became so deeply burdened that prayer began to occupy a major portion of his time. During the week, he would move down the aisle of the empty church and pray for the people who usually occupied each pew on Sunday.

The pastor persuaded the people of his church to clear the calendar of all other activities on Wednesday night so that they might dedicate themselves to prayer. On Sunday, he would tell his church, "If you have to miss a service, miss Sunday morning or evening. But don't miss Wednesday night." He stressed this until he saw attendance at prayer meeting increase from forty to one hundred twenty. There were also two children's prayer meetings with a total of forty in attendance. In all, one hundred sixty people out of a congregation of three hundred devoted themselves to prayer.

Next, the pastor invited his people to stay after church on Sunday evenings for a half hour of prayer. He then started cottage prayer meetings scattered throughout the city. The attendance was not large but momentum was growing. He set up a "prayer wheel," divided into fifteen minute segments twenty-four hours a day. He asked people to sign up, thus having at least one person praying around the clock. The deacons started meeting on Saturday nights to pray as long as they were led. They started at 9 P.M. and continued until they felt they had finished.

After two years of intensive prayer, a crusade led by Ralph and Lou Sutera began on Wednesday, October 13, 1971. The faithful gathered, expecting little or no response. Their doubts were confirmed when no one came forward to "get right with God" on the first night.

On the second night, God began to work in a prominent family in the church. Irma Derksen was one of the pillars of the church, along with her husband, Sam, a deacon. She had been praying for her church, her city, and her country while ignoring her own spiritually barren condition. She struggled under the heavy load of a critical spirit. There were people in the church whom she didn't like. She wouldn't even speak to Sam's brother, Arnold, who was also a deacon. Remarkably, Irma went forward that night, bowed at the altar, and faced up to the deadly sins that were destroying her inner life.

Irma accepted the fact that Christ had died on the cross to free her for her self-life. By faith, she claimed the power of the Holy Spirit. She left the altar radiant with joy. Her bitter spirit was broken. Rather than waiting for others to apologize to her, as was her custom, she initiated the conversations and asked for their forgiveness. For her, the Christian life was, as some would say, "a whole new ball game."[8]

Sam was unmoved by his wife's decision. His spiritual condition had waned to the point where he doubted that God even answered prayer. His thirteen-year-old feud with Arnold was so intense, so vitriolic, that they had not even spoken to one another for two years! The source of all this hatred started with a falling out over the music program of the church. Finally, Sam had lost all hope of being reconciled to Arnold.

One night, Arnold went to the basement for a meeting with the pastor and another deacon. Sam was invited to join them. Sam humbly said, "This feud has gone on long enough. I want to ask you to forgive me." "Well, it's about time," Arnold snapped back. His bitterness was just as evident as always.

The pastor and the other deacon prayed. They asked God for His mercy in healing this broken relationship between two brothers. They asked God to bring reconciliation. Arnold began to weep. "I've been wrong," he confessed. The brothers hugged each other, weeping and asking forgiveness. They returned to their waiting families and shared their renewed love. The next night, they sang a duet!

This broke the logjam. Pastor McLeod saw the inner life of his entire church transformed. The officers and teachers came forward to repent of their sins and restore their fellowship with God. The leadership of the church was a collection of broken people. It was as if the man-made structure of the church had crumbled. Pastor McLeod explained, "Then I saw God take that crumbled structure and build a real church, His church. It's beautiful to behold!"

Love permeated the congregation. Kurt Koch wrote about this transformation:

> McLeod told me in the course of a personal conversation, "The chief characteristic of this revival is love." People who previously could not stand one another have embraced each other and asked for forgiveness. Ministers have become reconciled with their coworkers. In all kinds of human relationships, the sand has been removed from the works. Love has become the basis upon which all questions are settled.[9]

What began as a meeting that was scheduled for twelve days turned into seven weeks. The crusade attendance overflowed at Ebenezer Baptist Church. There was a new love and unity in the whole Christian community, especially as the meetings were moved to larger churches to accommodate the crowds. Eventually twenty churches participated.

One attendee told Erwin Lutzer, "It was wonderful! . . . We were all packed into the church, and no one asked whether we were Baptist, Alliance, Mennonite, or whatever. We sensed intuitively that we were all part of the same body, the body of Christ."[10]

Conviction of sin and a determination to make restitution for past anger, bitterness, strife, dishonesty, and crime were demonstrated by many whose hearts had been touched. People returned to restaurants and hotels to confess and make restitution for bills they had long ignored. One man drove sixty miles to confess his sin and pay his debt to an insurance company he had defrauded. Young people confessed that they had taken drugs. With God's help they kicked the habit. Their parents repented of harshly judgmental attitudes toward their children.

One couple left the "afterglow meeting" at the church where people were praying for the needs of those who desired help. They were going home with their marital problems still unresolved. "Don't leave now," the leader exhorted, "or we'll pray that you have the worst night of your life."[11] The couple left anyway. At 1 A.M., they returned to surrender their lives and marriage to God. He was miraculously answering the prayers of many.

Kurt Koch asked Pastor McLeod, "Bill, what sort of sin was most frequently confessed?" He replied, "Arrogance, self-seeking, and pride."[12]

According to one estimate, at least three hundred people were converted through the witness of spiritually awakened believers. A fugitive criminal turned himself in to the police. A surprised official asked, "Why are you giving yourself up?" The criminal replied, "I have found the Lord Jesus here in your town and now I want to follow Him. That is why I am giving myself up."[13] This man's unusual honesty led to his release from the charges against him. He brought his wife and three children to the crusade. His wife, too, received Christ. The family was marvelously restored.

Andrew Murray declared, "The bond that unites a man to his fellow men is no less real and close than that which unites him to God; he is one with them. Grace renews not only our relation to God but to man, too. We not only learn to say 'My Father,' but 'Our Father.'"[14]

Our Lord heard the heart cry of Pastor McLeod and his church. In answer to their prayers Christ obviously manifested His presence and took charge. Then He displayed the power of His grace to change lives.

## Review Questions

1. Do you agree or disagree with the following statement? Why?

> Instead of the gospel turning the world upside down, the world is turning the church upside down, inside out, and every which way but loose!

2. What does a wrong view of liberty produce?
3. Do you agree or disagree with the following statement? Why?

> You can join nearly any church in America, liberal or conservative, without ever making a commitment to learn to obey all that Christ commanded.

4. Does your church gather together as God's people under the active headship of Christ? If not, why not?
5. Why do some churches lose their heavenly character, direction, and power?
6. What are the three passages in the New Testament that warn the church against following the bad example of the Israelites who died in the wilderness?
7. What is the starting point for the church to escape or avoid a deadly self-centered form of Christianity?
8. When do you feel like hiding from God? When do you run to God?
9. Does your church ever run from God? If so, why?
10. What would happen if families and congregations waited on God in prayer until the joy, hope, and holiness of Christ's presence was fully realized?
11. Whom do you strive to know face-to-face?
12. Can you share a time where you have seen God's glory?
13. What two indictments are leveled at the two churches mentioned in Revelation 2:4 and 3:15–16?
14. Read Acts 4:23–31. Instead of praying to escape persecution, for what did the early church pray? Why did the apostles rejoice when they were beaten for their loyalty to Christ?
15. What must happen in order for broken lives to be mended overnight, life-transforming power to be restored, the church to regain its rightful voice of moral authority and credibility, and the watching world to be drawn inexplicably to the Savior?

*Exercises*

1. Ask God in prayer to make known any sin that keeps you from knowing Christ intimately.
2. Meet with another member of your church and pray for God's glory to be seen in your congregation. Be sure to wait on God in prayer until the joy, hope, and holiness of Christ's presence is realized.

## CHAPTER SEVEN

# Asking Christ to Take Charge

ONE OF THE MOST important truths in this book is that God not only saves individuals but also churches and families. My prayers for my children and for my church were trapped in a web of doubt and unbelief until God opened my eyes to this truth. When I went to prayer for my children, I kept thinking, "They're in their teens now and I have no power or authority in prayer to prevail on God to transform their lives." WRONG!

I thought that salvation and godly living were such private individual matters that my prayers could have little or no influence on anyone other than myself. It is true that we are saved on an individual basis and that each person must trust in Christ. Godly living is also a choice that each one of us must make. No one can make that choice for us. However, prayer can powerfully influence a person's choices.

One day I discovered the amazing power of the headship of Christ over the church and also how His headship empowers parents, especially as they pray and labor to rear their children to know the Lord and wholly follow Him. I discovered why Paul passionately prayed that Christ might be fully formed not only in individuals but also in the Galatian churches (Gal. 4:19). Families and churches have a corporate life and character. Christ is not only the Head over individuals, but He is also "head over all things to the church" (Eph. 1:22). I learned that He seeks actively to take charge of all the details of our families and churches.

This truth led me to become a servant parent on duty for the

King and a shepherd consciously serving the church under Christ's immediate direction. It took a great load off of me and gave a new focus to my prayers. This is why I began to pray with Christ obviously present and actively in charge. This is how my faith was liberated so that I could pray in faith for our Lord to transform, not only me, but also my family and my church.

## Adam's Powerful Headship

To grasp the power of headship we must look at a negative example. Adam, the first man, demonstrates the incredible power of headship for good and for evil. Adam and Eve were created in the perfect image and likeness of God. Adam was Eve's head. Under his headship they lived in holiness and communion with God. They loved Him and one another completely. Their communion with God was perfect. They were of one mind and one heart with Him so that their fellowship with Him brought them great delight.

In this sinless state, Adam and Eve lived in perfect unity with God, and He was free to rule them in love. Their relationship of obedience to God was built on absolute love and trust. They faithfully fulfilled God's will on earth, for they delighted in pleasing Him. Their marriage was also harmonious, being totally free from conflict. In their lives together, Adam and Eve manifested the moral perfection of God's image. In a sense, their home was a colony of heaven on earth.

However, when the two sinned against God, their perfect unity with Him and their idyllic lives in the garden were shattered. Their lives were no longer mutually centered in God. Instead, both of them lived on the basis of their own *opinion* of what constituted good and evil. Thus, they promoted *self* as king of their lives, and the law of strife and conflict became the rule of life. Adam and Eve's marriage remained intact, but love and unity disappeared from their home.

Life became filled with sorrow, frustration, and emptiness. In their great "wisdom," Adam and Eve felt free to do whatever they pleased. In their spiritual naïveté, Satan had manipulated them into becoming his captives. A degenerate family and sin-cursed society emerged. Adam fathered sons and daughters in his own selfish likeness (Gen. 5:3). Figuratively, human beings became like fierce dogs, biting and destroying one another. For instance, Adam's first son, Cain, murdered his younger brother, Abel (4:8).

The awesome power of Adam's ruined headship locked the entire human race into this terrible bondage to selfishness and strife, dominated by the powerful, unseen presence of Satan. Since Adam, every human being has been born with a sinful nature, which alienates him or her from the life of God. This has led to total disaster. By Noah's day, violence filled the earth (6:13). The whole human race degenerated into such wickedness and corruption that God sent a worldwide flood that destroyed everyone but Noah and his family.

## The Powerful Headship of Grace

Noah stands in sharp contrast to Adam and the degenerate world resulting from his sin. Noah alone found grace in the eyes of the Lord, though he lived in an extremely perverse society. By faith, Noah built an ark that saved his entire family from the devastation of the worldwide flood (Heb. 11:7). In Noah, we see hope and deliverance. As the godly head of his family, he foreshadowed Christ who, by grace, would come and save individuals and families through His powerful headship. In Noah we see assurance that where sin abounded through Adam's fall, grace can much more abound through a godly, praying parent's headship. Grace is indeed far more powerful than sin (Rom. 5:20).

Satan worked through Adam to capture all his offspring. But in God's grace and mercy, He demonstrated that He could work through Noah to deliver his entire family from an extremely wicked society. Noah undoubtedly prevailed in prayer for his family. Later, Noah is cited as one of the devout saints in the Old Testament (Ezek. 14:14, 20). The power of prayer is not limited to fathers and their headship. Hannah's prayers successfully set Samuel apart to the Lord (1 Sam. 1:11). In the New Testament, Timothy came to faith through the prayers and godly example of his mother and grandmother (2 Tim. 1:5).

Of course, the power of headship working in grace to rescue us from the ruined life of Adam comes from Christ. As the Head over all things and over His body the church, the power of Christ's headship far surpasses and is infinitely greater than the headship of Adam, Noah, or anyone else.

Through the supreme power of Christ's headship, believers find freedom from self, Satan, and the world's wicked, strife-ridden society. We are not only set free from our past in Adam, but we are also anchored to our future in Christ (Heb. 6:18–20). We died to sin with Christ, who sets us free from sin's consuming power (Rom. 6:1–14). We share in the resurrection life of Christ (Gal. 2:20). He intercedes continually on our behalf in heaven at the right hand of the Father (Heb. 7:25). Bondage to sin, self, Satan, and the world no longer has to hold us as captives. Instead, we can now share Christ's supreme position of power and dominion over all the forces of evil (Eph. 1:19–23; 2:6).

## We Must Claim the Active Headship of Christ

Despite Christ's powerful headship, many individuals, families, and churches remain shackled to selfishness and strife. Christian marriages suffer from divorce at an alarming rate. A staggering number of churches collapse each year due to division and "splits." The world views this dilemma and concludes that our Lord is not really God, after all. Their unspoken question remains, "If God has rescued you Christians from the ruin of humanity's fall into sin, where is the evidence?" That's a sobering question!

The reason churches remain in bondage to selfishness and strife is because they neglect to unite the congregation in prayer. They are not *focused on keeping their union of love with Christ alive and growing.* The powerful church in Acts began as a prayer meeting in one accord. The people were focused on obeying Christ no matter what the cost, for they loved Him. After they prayed, they were all filled with the Spirit and shared amazing love for one another (Acts 1:14; 4:23–35). Christians must rediscover prayer meetings that restore and maintain our unity of love under the active headship of Christ. Many believers have utterly lost this vision.

A godly elder spent much time in private prayer and faithfully attended prayer meeting each week. However, he asked, "Pastor, why can't you give us a list of requests so that we could just pray at home and not need to make the trip to church for prayer meeting?"

If prayer meetings are solely for the purpose of distributing a list of prayer needs, then a list published in the bulletin could easily take the place of a prayer meeting. In thousands of churches, this is precisely what has happened. But united prayer means more than just asking God to answer a list of requests. United prayer focuses on keeping our love relationship with our Head alive and well. It binds our hearts together in one body under His leadership.

A team must meet with its coach and unite under his or her leadership. We possess an even closer and infinitely more powerful relationship with Christ. We are His body. We need to unite in prayer to share His active headship over us. Our Head stands fully ready to release among us all the wisdom, love, holiness, and power that His grace can provide. He desires to create and maintain a community on earth in union and communion with Himself. As such it is a colony of heaven on earth.

Through prayer the church clings to her Head, the Lord Jesus Christ. Any believer, any family, or any church can drift away from "holding fast to the Head, from whom all the body, nourished and knit together by joints and ligaments, grows with the increase that is from God" (Col. 2:19). Keeping this union of love is essential, for the Lord Jesus Christ alone is able to fill His church with His own life and power. He alone is able to take immediate control of our inner life, as well as our outward actions, and guide us.

Just as children share life and love with their parents, so the church family should share life and love with Christ. But though the union of life cannot be broken, the union of love can be neglected and even severed. This often happens in the parents' relationship with their children. Prodigal sons and daughters break their union of love with their parents. The union of life with their children remains intact, but parents are not free to give them their choice blessings.

The church that drifts away from its union of love with Christ grieves Him. Such a congregation cannot enjoy the mighty power of grace that works from His headship to perfect the union of love and holiness in the church. Congregations have a character and a life of their own. This is evident when we consider our Lord's warnings to the churches. For instance, the church in Ephesus left Jesus, its first love. He thus warned the believers in that congregation to repent, or He would judge them quickly (Rev. 2:4–5). A church without Jesus' light is facing spiritual death. The Laodicean church was spiritually lukewarm. Christ was outside and it had not even missed Him! He was ready to vomit that church out of His mouth, especially if it did not repent (3:16).

Prayer meetings in North America tend to focus on such things as the need for jobs, health, and increasing church attendance. We need to go beyond these surface needs and ask our Lord to be obviously present and actively in charge of our lives. We must be prepared to recognize by faith His presence and pour out our worship and love to Him. We need to read prayers of worship in the Bible and use them as models (Pss. 100; 145; 150; 1 Tim. 1:17; 6:15–16). Then we should unite in prayers that are focused on our love for the Lord and for one another (Ps. 116; Eph. 3:14–21; Phil. 1:9–11; 1 Thess. 3:11–13; 2 Thess. 3:5).

When Christians unite in prayer and endeavor to keep their union of love with Christ alive, well, and growing, they become sensitive to the lack of love in their fellowship and make the repairing of this love relationship a top priority. One pastor told of a time when he felt that the Spirit was grieved in his congregation when he preached on Sunday morning. That evening he sensed that the Spirit was still not free to bless the congregation.

He canceled his Sunday evening sermon and briefly explained what it means to grieve the Holy Spirit through various sins that have not been confessed and where no effort at restitution has been made. The pastor asked everyone to bow their heads. Then he said, "If you believe that you have grieved the Spirit, please raise your hand." Nearly every hand went up. That night the service ran late as people cleared their conscience before God and with one another. Then the blessing of God returned.

We must trust our Lord to take charge of us, and then we must become alert to every sin against His love and headship. My wife, Betty, and I began our courtship with extended times of prayer. We agreed that we would never be first in one another's life. We wanted to be lovers always, and we wanted our Lord Himself to be our supreme love.

By way of confession, I must tell you how the Lord was obviously actively in charge on one occasion after we had been married a few years. Early one Sunday morning I had sharp words with Betty before I left to go to the church to prepare my heart to preach. I started to pray, but words would not come out of my mouth. All I could think about was my wife. I tried to brush these thoughts aside, reasoning, "Oh, she's all right. She'll think nothing of it. She'll get over it. Well, there's really nothing to it."

All my brilliant reasoning got nowhere. I simply *could not pray* (1 Peter 3:7). Finally, I called home, saying, "I'm sorry for the way I talked to you. Will you forgive me?" Weeping, she choked out, "Yes." This "cleared the air." My freedom to pray and preach returned after I humbled myself, once again, with Christ actively in charge from His throne of grace.

## When Millions Prayed and Christ Was Obviously in Charge

At times, churches all over our country need a massive holy cleansing. The accumulation of unconfessed sins that have long grieved the Spirit have prevented the powerful headship of Christ from working in transforming grace. This was the case in the middle of the nineteenth century.

In 1857, churches were sliding downhill. Thousands of Americans were disillusioned with Christianity. William Miller, a New England farmer, had captured nationwide attention with his prediction that Christ would return on October 22, 1844. When nothing happened, many abandoned their faith. They were embittered and disillusioned.

America's moral and spiritual recovery began when Jeremiah Lanphier, a concerned layman, started a noon prayer meeting for New York businessmen. (Few women worked in stores and offices in those days.) Only six men came to the first prayer meeting on September 23, 1857. They met on the third floor of the "Consistory" of the Old Dutch Reformed Church on Fulton Street.

By spring, daily prayer meetings sprang up in many locations, and daily attendance grew to ten thousand. America's greatest spiritual awakening was under way. It was called the "Layman's Prayer Revival" because lay Christians led it.

During this time of unprecedented revival, the owner of a hardware store in New York urged business persons at the Fulton Street prayer meeting to set a holy example in all their practices. A well-known manufacturer followed him to his store and confessed that he had cheated him for years and wanted to pay back all that he had stolen.

When the news spread that there were daily prayer meetings where sinners were welcomed, prayed for, and encouraged to turn to Christ, some hardened criminals were saved. A notorious criminal named "Awful Gardiner" surprised everyone when he found Christ through the prayer meetings. He was not alone.

Hundreds of people who had always spent their nights in the gates of hell came to prayer meetings that had begun in the evenings. Thousands forsook crime and became devoted followers of Christ. Crime and vice drastically declined. Wealthy people generously helped the poor, whom they regarded as their brothers and sisters.

Ships coming into New York harbor came under the power

of God's presence. On one ship, a captain and thirty men were converted to Christ before the ship docked. Four sailors knelt for prayer in the depths of the battleship North Carolina, which was anchored in the harbor. They began to sing. This caused their ungodly shipmates to run down to make fun of them, but the power of God gripped them, and they humbly knelt in repentance.

A customer from Albany asked a New York City merchant, "Do you have to stop business at noon and go to a prayer meeting?" Without hesitation he replied, "Yes, I must. Why don't you go with me?" The customer went with him and trusted in Christ. He then returned to Albany and started prayer meetings there.

> Albany, the state capital, with 60,000 population, was the scene of unusal happenings. An early morning prayer meeting was initiated by state legislators who began with six participants in the rooms of the Court of Appeals opposite the Senate Chamber; soon asfterwards the rooms were overflowing. The noon prayer meetings attracted great crowds in Albany as elsewhere.[1]

It was reported that anyone traveling by horse and buggy from Omaha, Nebraska, to Washington, D.C., could count on finding a church packed for prayer at any place that they stopped along the way during any night of the week.

In December 1857, in Utica, New York, attendance at weekly union prayer meetings increased rapidly, so much so that by the third meeting the main floor and the balcony of the First Presbyterian Church were filled with deeply burdened people. Then daily prayer meetings were started each morning.

One night Dr. John L. Girardeaux dismissed the prayer meeting for spiritual awakening at Anson Street Presbyterian Church in Charleston, South Carolina, but no one left. The congregation stayed until midnight, and the Lord powerfully worked in their midst. Eight weeks of nightly meetings followed, reaching crowds numbering from fifteen hundred to two thousand. Many of these turned to the Lord in faith.

In the nation's capital,

> five daily prayer meetings were started, commencing
> respectively at 6:30 A.M., 10 A.M., 5 P.M., and 7 P.M., the
> YMCA and the churches sponsoring the effort. The
> capital's newspapers described the meeting as "still and
> solemn," and on April 1 commented editorially that the
> religious excitement in the city was unabated, five thou-
> sand or so attending the prayer service in the Academy
> of Music Hall in Washington. There was general con-
> sensus of opinion that a Divine visitation had occurred.[2]

The power of prayer touched every aspect of business. There
had never been a higher tone of honor. The Bible became the
standard. Any business that injured the community was regarded
as wrong. People in every kind of business began to be more
honest, truthful, and conscientious.

At least three thousand came to Christ in Newark, New Jersey. In many smaller towns scarcely any unconverted people
remained. In Haverhill, Massachusetts, the Spirit deeply moved
the crowded daily prayer meeting. Sometimes half of the assembly silently wept. One pastor found at least one person in every
home in his congregation deeply concerned about his or her
relationship with God.

An unsaved man was attending the prayer meetings on Fulton
Street in New York City, hoping that someone would help him.
None did. Then one day he heard a mother's written request
for her son's salvation. He discovered that the note was from
*his own mother!* Soon afterward he trusted in Christ.

In Kalamazoo, Michigan, a woman turned in a request for
her husband's salvation. One man responded, "Pray for me. I'm
that man." Four more men did likewise.

A wealthy young New Yorker was born again at a noon prayer
meeting. Upon returning home, he read from the Bible and knelt
to pour out a fervent prayer for his wife and sister. His wife and
sister knelt beside him and wept as they also received Christ.

One man disowned his daughter when she confessed Christ. However, when he fell deathly sick, he sent for her and asked her forgiveness. She shared Christ with him. Within three days, her father, mother, two brothers, and a sister entered the family of God.

Even Hell-Corner, New Hampshire, was touched. It all started when one man's outrageous profanity led to a joking call for a prayer meeting. A notorious backslider tried to lead but he broke down while praying. The meetings continued under the leadership of a man from another town, and four or five hardened men were convicted of sin and turned to Christ. A fresh breath from heaven was changing Hell-Corner.

In March, 1858, the voice of prayer and praise to God was heard beginning at 8:30 A.M. every morning in the halls of the New York state capitol. Six people began a prayer meeting for the legislature. By the fifth day, two rooms were filled and interest was growing.

Something equally momentous was taking place in New Jersey.

> By the month of March, the awakenings in New Jersey matched anything observed on the American continent. The city of Newark, population 70,000, witnessed startling evidences of a sweeping movement there. In a couple of months, 2,785 in all professed conversion, averaging one hundred conversions in each reporting congregation. It became a common sight to see business houses closed, with a notice "will reopen at the close of the prayer meeting," and the union meetings thus advertised were crowded to overflowing.[3]

Some of the leading businessmen of Boston were attending prayer meetings.

> By March 1858, the awakening in Boston (like its counterpart in New York City) had become news to the

whole nation. The Boston correspondent of a Washington newspaper affirmed that religion had become the chief concern in Boston and throughout New England. The meetings for prayer, he reported, were crowded and solemn, with the whole assembly sometimes in tears, under the melting power of the Spirit.[4]

When the churches were cleansed and began to humble themselves in prayer under the headship of Christ, mighty grace prevailed where sin had once abounded (Rom. 5:20). Someone said, "You don't have to defend a lion. All you have to do is let him out of his cage." This is true of the Lion of Judah! We need to ask the Head of the church to once again actively take charge of us.

## Review Questions

1. What is the highest calling that God can give any creature?
2. What qualities give convincing evidence to the world that our God is the only true and living God?
   a. our love for God
   b. our love for one another
   c. our unity with God
   d. our unity with one another
   e. all of the above
3. After sin entered the world through Adam and Eve, on what basis did they make their decisions?
4. Why does every person since Adam live in bondage to selfishness and strife, and experience domination by Satan?
   a. personal weakness
   b. lack of willpower
   c. Adam's headship
   d. bad luck of the draw
5. How did Noah prevail on behalf of his family?
6. Whose headship surpasses Noah, Adam, your dad, or anyone else?

7. For the Christian, why does bondage to sin, self, Satan, and the world no longer hold us captive?
   a. Christ's headship
   b. freedom from Adam's headship
   c. an eternal future in Christ
   d. death to sin
   e. all of the above
8. Why do some individuals, families, and churches remain shackled to selfishness and strife?
9. When the world sees a church split, what do they conclude?
10. What power goes largely untapped in overcoming all our sins, releasing us from every kind of bondage, and restoring us to complete unity with God and one another?
11. What's wrong with the usual prayer meeting?
12. What reasoning is lacking in this question: "Why can't we just pray at home?"
13. Name two benefits of united prayer.
14. Are there relationships in your family or church that need to be changed? Who are the specific people? How can you turn to Christ for His transforming power?
15. Do you feel that entire communities could be impacted by prayer today as they were in 1857–58? Why or why not?
16. Can you share how you have experienced a spiritual cleansing in your church or family?

*Exercises*

1. Meet with another member from your church and pray for Christ to transform your community, starting with your congregation.
2. Confess a broken relationship to the other involved person and seek to mend it through the power of Christ.

# FOURTH KEY:
## ASKING CHRIST TO CHANGE EACH OF US

*As many as I love, I rebuke and chasten. Therefore be
zealous and repent. (Rev. 3:19)*

## CHAPTER EIGHT

# Asking Christ to Change Each of Us

WE CANNOT MEET IN prayer with Christ without humbly expecting our sinless Lord and Savior to change us in order to make us holy. The Bible calls this radical change repentance. What exactly does "repentance" mean? The word comes from the Greek term *metanoia*. It refers to

> the change of mind of those who have begun to abhor their errors and misdeeds, and have determined to enter upon a better course of life, so that it embraces both a recognition of sin and sorrow for it and hearty amendment, the tokens and effects of which are good deeds.[1]

When we unite in prayer, we need to ask our Lord to change each one of us as He sees fit. The Bible calls the change we seek *repentance*. Reconciliation with a holy God and a growing intimate relationship of love with Him require two things. We must respond to Him with faith and repentance. Faith and repentance are like two sides of a coin. You can distinguish them but you cannot separate them.

One man wisely shared, "I repented before I knew what repentance was, and I have repented many times since." He was unusual, for the average American Christian does not understand why he or she should ever repent, let alone repent repeatedly.

Today we have forgotten our need to repent not only of our personal sins but also of the sins of the church. When our Lord calls

His church to repent, it includes *every believer* (Rev. 2:5, 16, 21, 22; 3:3, 19). We are members of the church, the body of Christ, so when the body sins, we all sin.

Isaiah was a faithful prophet, but consider his cry after he saw the Lord in His glory and majesty. "So I said: 'Woe is me, for I am undone! Because I am a man of unclean lips, and I dwell in the midst of a people of unclean lips; for my eyes have seen the King, the LORD of hosts'" (Isa. 6:5). Isaiah repented not only because of his own personal sins, but also because of his identification with the backslidden people of God.

We are prone to think that repentance needs to begin in the dens of iniquity among those who are grossly sinful. But in reality Christians need to repent first, for God's judgment always begins with His own people. "For the time has come for judgment to begin at the house of God; and if it begins with us first, what will be the end of those who do not obey the gospel of God?" (1 Peter 4:17). When God pours out His righteous indignation on America, He will begin with the church! Why is this the place to begin?

## Our Neglected Responsibility

The church has the responsibility to shine as lights in the midst of a perverse generation (Phil. 2:15). America has turned away from the Scriptures and from God. As a nation, we have wallowed in the darkest forms of immorality. This is due in large measure to the fact that *the Christian community fails to shine as lights*.

Our love relationship with Christ and with one another has waned considerably. We are like the church of Ephesus. The members of that first-century congregation had performed many good works for God but they had departed from Christ, their first love. Jesus warned, "Remember therefore from where you have fallen; repent and do the first works, or else I will come to you quickly and remove your lampstand from its place—unless you repent" (Rev. 2:5). When the light of God's presence is removed from the church, society quickly degenerates to the lowest depths of pagan darkness.

When our Lord calls the church to repent, even the "best" members are individually and collectively responsible to heed the call. The church desperately needs to unite today in an outpouring of repentant prayer. We need to repent and return to Christ with complete love and devotion, no matter what the cost.

The church in America also bears an awesome responsibility for the extreme moral depravity dominating our country today, for we have neglected God's command to pray for all people, especially for all who are in authority (1 Tim. 2:1 8).

How extremely important this is! God has empowered us to wage effective warfare and to use prayer to restrain the invisible powers of evil (Eph. 6:10–20). Satan seeks to control our country by dominating our officials. God calls us to wage war by praying against the unseen "rulers of the darkness of this age, against spiritual hosts of wickedness in the heavenly places" (v. 12). Failure to pray as warriors facing the enemy in battle is like the desertion of soldiers from their place on the firing line.

Both churches and individual Christians face the responsibility to repent of our neglect of waging spiritual warfare through prayer. We should be like Daniel. In Daniel 9, the prophet-statesman confessed the sins of Israel. The moral purity of his own life was such that his enemies could find no fault in him. Nevertheless, he accepted the responsibility to confess and repent of the sins of his people.

Christians in Romania are actually called "repenters" because evangelical pastors have preached repentance. In fact, the revival that came to Romania has been attributed to the wave of repentance that swept through the churches in response to the call to repent. These "repenters" are known for their remarkable commitment. If two hundred Romanian evangelicals come to church on Sunday morning, then the same two hundred will attend Sunday night and again Wednesday night for prayer meeting. These repenters demonstrate unusual zeal for reaching the lost. They stand in the aisles at evangelistic meetings so that unsaved friends may have a seat. In frigid weather, they even stand outside to free up space inside for the unconverted.

## Repentance in the Early Church

Repentance is at the heart of our gospel message. The early church preached repentance constantly. Peter's sermon in Acts 2 confronted the crowd gathered in Jerusalem with the shocking fact that they were guilty of crucifying their own Messiah. Nevertheless, God raised Him from the dead. Peter boldly concluded his sermon with these words:

> "Therefore let all the house of Israel know assuredly that God has made this Jesus, whom you crucified, both Lord and Christ." Now when they heard this, they were cut to the heart, and said to Peter and to the rest of the apostles, "Men and brethren, what shall we do?" Then Peter said to them, "Repent, and let every one of you be baptized in the name of Jesus Christ for the remission of sins; and you shall receive the gift of the Holy Spirit. For the promise is to you and to your children, and to all who are afar off, as many as the Lord our God will call." (Acts 2:36–39)

Convinced that God had, in fact, raised Jesus from the dead and made Him both Lord and Christ, the listeners were ready to repent of crucifying Him and risk persecution by openly putting their trust in Him. Once they believed the message that Christ had actually been raised from the dead and seated in the place of supreme power at the Father's right hand, turning to Jesus in repentance and faith was the only reasonable response.

Peter's listeners found themselves in the same position as Joseph's brothers. Remember the account in Genesis about how his brothers despised him and sold him into slavery? Years afterward they discovered that God had exalted him to the highest position of authority in Egypt, second only to Pharaoh himself. Joseph, whom his brothers had cruelly rejected and betrayed, now sat enthroned in power. He held the keys of life and death over them. Smitten with awe, these brothers knew that they desperately needed Joseph's mercy and forgiveness. Obviously the discovery of his exaltation to great power and authority resulted in their repentance.

We need to proclaim Christ risen and exalted. This message calls for repentance. However, proclaiming the gospel in our country today almost universally stops with the death of Christ and fails to focus on His exaltation to the throne of supreme power and authority. We need to preach Christ on the cross *and* on the throne. This truth requires all people everywhere to repent (Acts 17:30).

The late Martin O. Massinger, former president of Dallas Bible College and a member of a mission board, offered unusual wisdom on this point. He told me that when he asked missionary candidates to explain the gospel, they usually failed to declare Christ's present power. Inevitably, they would stop with the death of Christ, making no mention of His resurrection and His present position of authority and power at the right hand of the Father. They obviously believed in these truths, but they failed to see the importance of confronting the unsaved with Jesus' supreme power and authority.

Preaching Christ's death and resurrection tells *part* of the good news. However, we must make clear His present position of supreme power and thus the need for everyone to repent by turning to Him from their sins and idols. Sadly, the teachings of the church today often appear "fuzzy" at best concerning repentance.

## Repentance and Faith

Repentance is not a good work that we do for God. Rather, He grants contrition as His gift to us. According to Acts 11:18, God has granted "repentance to life" to both Jews and Gentiles. Repentance and faith are inseparably one.

The conversion of Saul of Tarsus serves as an example of faith and repentance. He persecuted Christians because he was convinced that Jesus was not the Messiah (or Christ). Because Paul was a devout Jew, serving God meant crushing Christianity's departure from Judaism. The Pharisee set his sights on annihilating followers of the Way (9:1–2).

When Saul met Jesus on the road heading to Damascus, he suddenly knew that he had been wrong. The truth that Jesus arose from the dead and now has all power in heaven and earth demanded a complete about-face, that is, a total change for Saul. He repented and trusted in Jesus for salvation. This dramatic change caused him to risk his own life by preaching in the synagogues that Christ truly is the Son of God (vv. 20–25).

Throughout the rest of Acts, we read of Saul (later called Paul) suffering persecution because he preached Christ. This ex-Pharisee, who had once despised Jewish and Gentile Christians, spent years in jail because he insisted that "Gentiles should be fellow heirs, of the same body, and partakers of His promise in Christ through the gospel" (Eph. 3:6). Paul refused to tolerate the attempts of some Hebrew Christians to assign second-class status to Gentile believers. As a repenter, Paul taught the churches he had established to repent and accept the new equality of both Jews and Gentiles in the body of Christ (Gal. 3:28).

Everywhere that believers proclaimed the gospel, repentance radically changed the lives of sinners. At Thessalonica, the cry raised against Paul and his companions attests to their fervor and effectiveness in evangelizing the lost. "These who have turned the world upside down have come here too" (Acts. 17:6). The Thessalonian church experienced complete repentance in response to Paul's preaching.

> For they themselves declare concerning us what manner of entry we had to you, and how you turned to God from idols to serve the living and true God, and to wait for His Son from heaven, whom He raised from the dead, even Jesus who delivers us from the wrath to come. (1 Thess. 1:9–10)

So many turned away from idolatry in Ephesus that idol makers feared for their financial lives. Their businesses were threatened with bankruptcy (Acts 19:23–29).

## The Great Need of the Hour

Obviously the church in North America comes short regarding this kind of life-changing witness. Warren Wiersbe speaks to this issue in his book entitled *The Integrity Crisis.*

> For nineteen centuries, the church has been telling the world to admit its sins, repent, and believe the gospel. Today, in the twilight of the twentieth century, the world is *telling the church to face up to her sins, repent, and start being the true church of that gospel.* We Christians boast that we are not ashamed of the gospel of Christ, but perhaps the gospel of Christ is ashamed of us. For some reason, our ministry doesn't match our message. Something is wrong with the church's integrity. The church has grown accustomed to hearing people question the message of the gospel, because that message is foolishness to the lost. But today the situation is embarrassingly reversed, for now the messenger is suspect. Both the ministry and the message of the church have lost credibility before a watching world, and the world seems to be enjoying the spectacle. "Why should we listen to the church?" the critical world is asking. "By what authority do you Christians preach to us about sin and salvation? Set your own house in order and then we may want to listen to you."[2]

Some Christians recognize this need for repentance. Look at what happened when one church earnestly prayed for Christ to take charge and change them. Betty and I visited Birchman Baptist Church on the west side of Fort Worth in November 1988. A crusade led by the late Del Fehsenfeld Jr. and his Life Action Team was bringing the message of repentance "home" to the people. A lady sitting next to us confided, "This church has had a cleansing like I have never seen before." Pastor Miles Seaborn agreed. He wrote the following:

> God touched down at Birchman Baptist Church, and we have experienced revival in a way never before known in the eighty-five year history of our church. Hundreds of individual lives have been changed, marriages have been restored or revitalized, immorality in all its forms has been confessed and repented of, . . . and restitution of thousands of dollars has been made to former employers, IRS, family members, companies, banks, hospitals, etc. These have been broken before the Lord, have publicly confessed their sins, and are experiencing the continuing joy of forgiveness and an obedient life. They are reaching out in love to each other and to others in and out of the church. Every age group has been touched, but the intensity and focus of revival seems to have centered on our singles and young married adults and families.[3]

Pastor Seaborn shared a few examples of what God had done. A beauty operator said, "The night Del preached on divorce nearly wiped me out! I told my husband when we got home, if I had known Jesus like I know Him now, I would never have divorced my first husband. But since I can't do anything about that now, I just want you to know that you're *never* going to get rid of me! I will *never* leave you."

A father confessed to the congregation, "When we knelt to pray just now about bitterness, I thought that I didn't have any bitterness in my heart. Then the face of my son appeared before me. I have taken him to the prayer room and asked forgiveness for the excessive discipline I've given him all of his life for just being a normal little boy. You see, I was married sixteen and a half years ago, and he was born sixteen years ago. All of his life, I have blamed him for ruining my life."

A deacon broke down and admitted, "Seven years ago I was in an adulterous situation. Brother Miles found out and told me that I had to tell my wife and ask forgiveness from the church, which I did in a noncommittal way. I was bitter at Brother Miles for five years, but tonight God spoke to me and I had to take my wife outside during the service and confess to her that it did not end seven years ago. I realized that *pride* has been at the root of my moral impurity all my adult life, and tonight—the hardest thing I ever did, some of my best friends may never speak to me again—I *had* to come up here and confess publicly that I have sinned against God, my family, and this church, and I want to ask for your forgiveness."

A young businessman and Sunday school teacher humbly acknowledged, "My life was like the fake Rolex watch that I wore. It looks good on the outside, but inside there is nothing of value."

According to Pastor Seaborn, this man "went back to all of his family members, including a favorite uncle from whom he had stolen, to former employers, and his former commanding officer to confess and make restitution for the wrongs he had committed. Just this week, he was rocking his baby and feeling good about a clear conscience when the Lord reminded him that he had one more thing to clear up. He had lied on his application to General Dynamics when he applied and was accepted for a five-security-level job. In obedience, he has gone back to his supervisor and confessed this sin. He knew he might lose his job or even go to jail, but was willing to take the chance in order to be clear before God."

A seminary student declared, "I have been addicted to pornography since I was a young boy. I have asked God's forgiveness, my wife's forgiveness, and I want to ask the church's forgiveness."

One man wrote the Oklahoma State University bookstore, confessing he that had stolen three hundred dollars worth of books plus a calculator eight years earlier while he was a student. He returned the money and asked their forgiveness. This was such a surprise to the unbelieving world that television news, *USA Today*, and other newspapers reported it.

Couple after couple have shared how God has restored their love for each other. They now have an openness in communication that they have never before experienced and a oneness of spirit that they have never known, along with a desire to share their lives with others.

Many shared the spirit of one who said, "The Lord has brought to the surface some deep-rooted evidences of pride that have been stifling the power of God in my life. I have asked God to give me the grace to adopt the attitude of Christ that I should have, as described in Philippians 2:5–8."

This remarkable work of the Spirit was an answer to intensive prayer, which began two years earlier. The church prayed and fasted every Saturday for six weeks preceding the crusade. Women prayed and shared for two hours one morning each week. The men met for prayer at 7 A.M. daily.

Prayer continued during the crusade. Hundreds went to the prayer room to meet God about issues they needed to make right. One night, two hundred joined the Life Action Team in prayer from 11 P.M. until 2 A.M.

Eight years later, Pastor Seaborn said the impact of that revival was continuing. Birchman Baptist is a praying church where many committed prayer warriors intercede daily, expecting the Lord to change lives. From this we see that when we unite in prayer, we need to trust the Lord to change each one of us as He sees fit.

## Review Questions

1. Reconciliation with a holy God and a growing relationship of love with Him requires two things. Name them.
2. Describe the change that occurred in Job's life, as recorded in chapter 42 of the book bearing his name.
3. Isaiah repented for two reasons. Why?

4. Name two examples from the Old Testament of people who accepted the responsibility of confessing the sins of their people.
5. Describe repentance in your own words.
6. Do you agree or disagree with the following statement? Why?

> Repentance is not a good work that we do for God.

7. Identify the issues in your family or church that need repentance.
8. How have you seen the power of Christ through the repentance of others?
9. What would you like to see happen in your church or family related to revival?
10. Do you believe that America has embraced the darkest immorality? Why or why not?
11. What happens when the church fails to shine as light?
    a. It generates no heat.
    b. Society quickly degenerates to the lowest depths of pagan darkness.
    c. The lost remain unregenerate.
    d. The church degenerates to the lowest depths.
12. What must happen before churches in North America can effectively call our adulterous society to repentance?
13. Do you agree or disagree with the following statement from Warren Wiersbe? Why or why not?

> We Christians boast that we are not ashamed of the gospel of Christ, but perhaps the gospel of Christ is ashamed of us.

15. Has Christ remained your first love? How is this demonstrated in your normal day?

*Exercises*

1. Make a weekly schedule to pray for the people in leadership in your church, community, state, and country. Pray
   with your family for those on the schedule.
2. Meet with a member of your church and focus in prayer
   and confession on those areas of your congregation that
   need repentance.
3. We invite you to visit Bible Prayer Fellowship on the web
   (www.praywithChrist.org) for news of meetings focused on
   prayer for spiritual awakening, and also review the *Leader's
   Guide for Praying with Christ Obviously Present and Actively
   in Charge.*

## CHAPTER NINE

# Christ Disciplines His Church

AN EX-PASTOR, YOUTH PASTOR, six elders, two other moderators, and I were seated around a table. We had met to reconcile the ex-pastor and the elders. "I have no special ability to restore harmony among you," I began. "However, I am convinced that the Lord Jesus Christ is able to take His place in our midst as the great Reconciler. He is able to unite us all in faith, love, and obedience. Let's unite in claiming the promise of His presence in Matthew 18:19–20. In this passage, Jesus gives us this powerful assurance, 'Again I say to you that if two of you agree on earth concerning anything that they ask, it will be done for them by My Father in heaven. For where two or three are gathered together in My name, I am there in the midst of them.'"

I outlined the steps by which we would discuss the points of conflict and pause for prayer at any time that any of us felt the need to do so. We all knew that only the Lord could heal the strife that had broken out between them. We were not disappointed. After the group had some lengthy discussions and paused twice for prayer, one man broke the ice by asking the ex-pastor to forgive him. Then the pastor asked forgiveness, and so did everyone else. The meeting closed by singing in heavenly harmony "Blest Be the Tie That Binds."

In Matthew 18:19–20, Jesus promised to be in the midst of believers gathered together in His name for prayer. Verses 15–18 are about unresolved conflicts and sin in the church. Christ promised to be present to resolve conflicts and restore sinning brothers. Verses 17–18 recognize that a stubbornly unrepentant person would have to be separated from the fellowship of the church until he or she repented. This is remedial church discipline.

Some folks think that Jesus would never discipline the unrepentant, but this passage shows that they are mistaken. He promised to be present to take charge of discipline. If ever there was a time when Christians needed to pray together and claim the presence of Christ, it is when people must be reconciled, restored, or disciplined.

It's obvious that those who unite in prayer must be in harmony with our Father in heaven throughout this whole procedure. The purpose is not to put the backslider permanently out of the church but to restore him or her to a true relationship with our heavenly Father and His family. Even removing wayward believers from Christian fellowship aims to wake them up and restore them to the congregation.

Effective discipline, which eventually restores those who have gone astray, means work—and lots of it. I have read Matthew 18:15–20 to couples on the verge of divorce and claimed the presence of Christ to restore their relationship. In one case, I prayed, counseled, and pursued fulfillment of this promise for eighteen months before reconciliation came. This promise brings great encouragement, especially as we depend on the presence of Christ in our midst to do a supernatural work of reconciling love in answer to our prayers.

Matthew 18:15–20 is about the divine government of our churches, our homes, and our small groups. United prayer in this case is claiming the government of God over the local church with its families and small groups. Thus we create a place of refuge from the evil powers of darkness. "The name of the LORD is a strong tower; the righteous run into it and are safe" (Prov. 18:10).

When Christians are disobedient, they move out from under this protection and expose themselves to the attacks of the Devil. They become like straying sheep who wander away from the shepherd's protection and roam where wolves and lions wait to devour them. Through prayer in one accord, straying believers are restored to safety under God's protective authority.

In our fallen world where Satan has usurped so much power, a "safe community" where believers pray together is an absolute necessity. Here those who go astray may be restored. God provided a similar refuge in Israel.

God was present in the Old Testament tabernacle (and later in the temple) to establish a protective government for His people. The tabernacle was God's house of prayer, and it was also the seat of divine government (Exod. 25:8, 22). When conflicts arose, people could go to the temple to let God resolve the matter (2 Chron. 6:22-23). If the nation suffered from famine, pestilence, or defeat in war because they had sinned, they could pray toward the temple, confess their sins, and trust God to forgive them (vv. 24-40).

Just as children have a common meeting place in their parents, so God's people have to know the Lord as their common meeting place and expect to experience Him ruling over them in grace. The only thing worse than personally falling into sin is to discover that the divine government has been removed from the place of worship. This is what happened to Israel when God withdrew His presence from the temple. The cloud of glory departed (Ezek. 11:22-23). The Babylonians eventually destroyed the sanctuary and carried the people of Judah into captivity. There was no longer a place where God made His home and provided a refuge for a righteous community.

Jesus' instructions in Matthew 18:15-20 tell believers today how to maintain discipline under the immediate direction and control of Christ. When they heed His teaching, they become a community where discipline is maintained and God is known as a refuge for the obedient. We must be diligent in prayer to claim this divine discipline. Without it we are like sheep who have no shepherd.

A key factor in effective discipline requires us to convince the people that they are dealing with the Lord Jesus Christ Himself, not just a mere human. To achieve this goal, the praying group must let God search their hearts and cleanse them from all self-righteousness, pride, and any other sins. We must truly pray in

Jesus' name and act as His representatives. Furthermore, the praying group must act with confidence, truly believing that the Savior indeed is in their midst and ready to work in supernatural grace and power.

The group needs to tell the erring one(s) that they are claiming this promise of Christ's presence. I have seen an emphasis on His presence make an extraordinary difference in the way people respond. I have seen divided churches and broken marriages begin to heal when Matthew 18:15–20 is read and the repentant claim Christ's presence as their head. They sincerely pray for Him to actively taking charge of them. It is not necessary for the pastor or elders to serve as peacemakers. Any believer can serve as peacemaker and restore the wayward.

## The Necessity of Church Discipline

Discipline in the church is absolutely essential, for without it the church tolerates sin and courts the possible loss of Christ's presence in its midst. A church lacking scriptural discipline bathed in prayer eventually becomes spiritually powerless and chaotic.

On one occasion, I was leading a large group of unruly junior boys in a suburban church. They had absolutely no interest in spiritual things. Their language and bad habits told me that they were more interested in acting like "tough guys." Worse yet, they were imitating some of the church leaders who were bad examples. I told a godly deacon, "We need some discipline in this church." He agreed but confessed, "We'd have to begin with my daughter, and I don't know who'd be left."

This response is all too common. For example, let's consider the following discussion in a pastor's meeting. "What do you do with a church member who you know is committing adultery?" a young pastor asked a group of ministers. Silence followed. "You'd better leave him alone," an older experienced minister finally warned. "If you make an issue of it, you'll split your church. Take my advice; leave him alone." Further conversation disclosed that this group of ministers were not shocked. They simply did not know how to deal with this common problem.[1]

People fear that discipline will divide or possibly destroy the church when, in reality, the opposite is true. Wise biblical discipline will unite the church, revive its spirit, and produce solid growth in its members.

Dean Kelley, an executive with the National Council of Churches, wrote a book entitled *Why Conservative Churches are Growing.* His conclusion boils down to two things. High membership requirements and the exercise of church discipline produces growth. Compared with liberal churches, some conservative churches may have a bit of discipline left. Nevertheless, an alarming number of churches faithfully teach the Bible but literally run from church discipline as they would the plague.

Like Samson of old, these congregations are drifting away from their commitment to love and obey the Lord. Samson drifted down this path until he completely abandoned his devotion to God. Finally, he gave up his long hair, which was the sign of his vow of faithful obedience to God at any cost. Tragically, after Delilah cut his hair, he was no longer God's mighty warrior. Even more tragically, we read, "But he did not know that the LORD had departed from him" (Judg. 16:20). Suddenly, the power of God was withdrawn, and Samson was no stronger than any other man. The once great warrior of God's enemies immediately became their pitiful captive.

Though Christ will not depart from individual believers today, His power may be withdrawn from those who lead undisciplined lives. But the broader issue has to do with the church. Can Christ leave a local church? Indeed He can! He left the Laodicean church (Rev. 3:14–22). Outwardly, this church functioned with great success, but inwardly their spiritual power was gone. They never even missed Christ's departure. They had left total dependence and loyalty to Christ far behind. Disgusted with them, Christ threatened to vomit them out of His mouth if they did not repent (v. 16).

There's no such thing as eternal security for local churches.

The Lord doesn't reside within a church just because we invoke His name. He knows where He's no longer wanted.

Christ's withdrawal takes place gradually. Because of this, our awareness of His presence and power fades, as well. He eventually becomes a mere figurehead. Over the course of time, the church loses the power to rebuke sin with boldness. The unruly crowd opposes righteousness. In its blundering way, the church mistakenly thinks that it must have their support. The high standards of righteousness are forgotten and the church backslides.

This is not the way God intends it, nor does it have to be this way. God will prove Himself faithful in the midst of true church discipline. I have seen Him do it numerous times. For example, a young couple in a church where I was pastor had fallen into sexual sin a few weeks before I married them. The early birth of their baby made this abundantly clear for all to see.

When I confronted the couple privately, they fumed with belligerence. The husband angrily snarled, "We'll just have to get another church!" "Go ahead," I replied. "I'm not begging you to stay. But I'll tell you one thing. The God of Jonah knows how to find you and deal with you. It'll go easier if you take the discipline we give you." Suddenly, he became humble and apologetic, asking, "What can we do?"

I explained, "You have tarnished the marriage standards of the church, and the young people who realize what you've done need to know that you have repented. Repenting calls for making a public apology. You need not go into details about your sin, but rather confess that you have not allowed Christ to be the Lord of your lives." Their changed attitudes showed that they had come to heartfelt repentance. They wanted Christ restored to His rightful place of authority in their marriage, and agreed to publicly repent, saying, "We will."

At the Sunday morning service, this couple fulfilled their promise. Those who knew what had happened got the message. Eventually the couple moved away. Many years later I heard a knock on the church door while I was studying. I opened the door and there was this same man. He had returned to thank me for the discipline.

## The Purpose of Church Discipline

Church discipline has two principal purposes. *First, it preserves the character of the church. The church must keep her purity and loyalty to Christ.* The Bible paints a portrait of the church as the "bride of Christ." She lives in a world totally alienated from God and vehemently at war with Him. The church's faithfulness to Christ means death to the world. But neutrality in this conflict represents disloyalty to Christ.

Our Lord told the church in Laodicea, "Therefore be zealous and repent" (Rev. 3:19). Zeal means passionate jealousy, the kind that makes your face flush with godly indignation. It's the way that any decent husband would feel if he saw his wife out with another man.

We serve a "jealous" God. Jealous is His name (Exod. 34:14). He does not tolerate His people's flirtations with pagan deities. He must reign absolutely supreme in the lives of His people. Elijah proved himself "jealous" for the restoration of God's honor and glory by seeking to destroy Baal worship in Israel. Jesus displayed intense "jealousy" for God's honor when He cleansed the temple, and He paid for this act with His life! Paul watched over the churches with "jealousy," saying, "For I have betrothed you to one husband, that I may present you as a chaste virgin to Christ" (2 Cor. 11:2).

*The second purpose for church discipline is to preserve the spiritual the life of the backslider.* In addition to preserving the character of the church, Paul also said that discipline was for the good of the individual. He called for the excommunication of the immoral believer "that his spirit may be saved in the day of the Lord Jesus" (1 Cor. 5:5).

Church discipline saves the lives of believers by restoring them to obedience, which is their only place of safety. True salvation means escaping from the cruel kingdom of Satan, thereby finding protection under the gracious rule of Christ. Israel fled from the terror of Pharaoh's dreaded throne and found protection under the rule of God (through Moses). In a similar manner, the Christian finds deliverance from the power of darkness by entering into the kingdom of God's Son (Col. 1:13).

Even so, those who belong to the kingdom of Christ can stray by choosing to obey Satan rather than God, just like disobedient Israel. A disobedient believer has returned to the tyrant. He belongs to Christ but has once again pitched his tent in enemy territory. In this precarious position, he faces spiritual danger, hunger, and grave loss of eternal rewards.

Lot gives us a sad illustration of this. Money and prestige lured him to Sodom, thereby costing him his wife as she fell victim to God's judgment upon the city. All Lot's possessions were burned, his daughters lost their purity, and his earthly accomplishments were lost. In fact, Lot forfeited virtually everything. But he escaped the judgment of God because of the prayers of Abraham.

Like Lot, the disobedient believer needs deliverance from the peril into which he has strayed. Like sheep without a shepherd, he alone faces the enemies of his soul. This is true loneliness! Disobedience leads him *into* danger, while discipline delivers him *from* danger.

Quite often a word of admonition proves sufficient to deliver a believer from selfishness. Dr. Howard Hendricks recalls a professor at Wheaton College who transformed his life with a timely rebuke. In *Say It With Love*, Hendricks writes, "I came out of that office so mad that I could spit nails. But today I call this man blessed because he's the only one who cared enough about me to face me with hard facts about my stubborn self-will. I made a 180-degree turn that I'm still following."[2]

Even in the rare case where discipline reaches the point of putting a believer out of the church fellowship, the purpose is still to save his or her soul. The immoral man excommunicated from the church in 1 Corinthians 5 had repented by the time Paul wrote 2 Corinthians. The apostle promptly urged the church to take him back (2 Cor. 2:5–11). Discipline ran its course for the good of all.

## Where Does Discipline Begin?

Exactly what sins call for discipline? Suppose a man wears obnoxious ties? What if a church member gets a speeding ticket? What about girls who dress immodestly? Would your church discipline a man convicted of fraud? Suppose he writes a hot check? What if he sues his wife for divorce? What about people who gossip? Suppose a member misses church for a month without good reason?

Questions like these have troubled various congregations whenever the subject of discipline arises. Lists of major and minor sins have been drawn up, meting out appropriate discipline. Inconsistencies have developed over these issues, with some leaders majoring on a few pet sins while ignoring others altogether. Sometimes petty faultfinding sets in. This obviously is not the basis for handling church discipline, for the approach misses the target.

Marlin Jeshke, in a book entitled *Discipling the Brother*, gives an entirely different viewpoint. A believer who falls into sin also falls into unbelief. He is ceasing to trust Christ according to the gospel. He is departing from the living God in unbelief (Heb. 3:12). As Jeshke put it, "if response to the gospel is the condition of admission of persons into the church—and there surely what decides is not the kind or size of a man's sin but his repentance for it—then response to the gospel must also remain the condition for the continuation of persons in the church."[3]

For Jeshke, restoring a brother to obedience to the Lord and winning the lost are quite similar. Both the lost and the backslider are living under the rule of the enemy, and both need deliverance. When dealing with the lost, there is no distinction between the drunk and the self-righteous, moral man. Both are lost, and both need Christ.

Claiming Christ's presence in our midst when we pray for straying sheep keeps discipleship and discipline centered on Him. The goal, as always, is to make Christ preeminent in every believer, in our homes, in our fellowship groups, and in our churches. Paul passionately prayed to this end, namely, that Christ would be fully formed in the Galatian churches (Gal. 4:19).

We approach discipline in this same spirit. As soon as we see a person drifting from the joy of Christ's fellowship, we must seek to restore him by praying for him. We start by praying that every believer may live to the praise of God's glory (Eph 1:12, 14). We also pray that Christ might be completely "at home" in the hearts of all who are called by His name (Eph. 3:17).

In reality, some Christians are prodigals who have fallen into lust for every conceivable sin. Others, like the self-righteous elder brother, attend church every time the doors open. Both types stand in desperate need of repentance, and neither has the joy of the Lord.

The issue in church discipline does not depend on the severity or seriousness of the sin, but on whether repentance has taken place. Is the person walking with God *now*? Discipline aims to produce repentance, restore fellowship, and make a believer spiritually stable. Under the guidance of the Spirit, the church must give whatever discipline may be required to accomplish these objectives.

## The Matter of Loving Support

Sometimes we need to give loving support rather than strong rebuke. Knuteson tells of Vicky, a young divorcée, struggling to support her two children. Child support checks came infrequently, and her income failed to cover the bills.

One day, under this pressure, she forged a company check. She faced arrest, and the story hit the headlines of the local newspaper. The prospects for her future and that of her children looked bleak, putting it mildly. Fortunately, she had the loving support of some sensitive fellow believers who came to her aid. With their help, she repaid the entire amount. These Christians testified in court to her generally good character, especially that she was not addicted to this kind of activity. Thanks to the help of her friends, she now lives in victory. No other discipline was necessary.[4]

The goal is always the same. As coworkers with God, we aim

to lift the fallen believer out of the pit and set his feet back on the rock. We want to help put a new song in his mouth, even praise to our God, and establish his conduct in righteousness (Ps. 40:1–3).

How do we reach this goal? We must claim the Lord's presence, especially as we pray that He will take charge of us and fill us with "the knowledge of His will in all wisdom and spiritual understanding" (Col. 1:9). Redemptive church discipline means catching the vision of making disciples of all believers in the spirit of Christ's love.

Wise discipline in an environment of love makes children secure, for they know their boundaries. It does this for the church family as well. One man said we are like a rescue team picking up people who have gone over a cliff and crashed below. We also are building a disciplined community at the top to keep others secure within the boundaries so that they and their families will not crash. We join together, praying for Christ's power to change lives in a disciplined community.

## Review Questions

1. Name the three steps of church discipline, according to Matthew 18:15–17.
2. A key factor in effective discipline requires us to convince sinning believers that they
   a. really are a sinner?
   b. are dealing with the Lord Jesus Christ Himself, not mere people?
   c. may not be saved at all?
   d. are a bad example?
4. Why is church discipline necessary?
   a. Without discipline, it means that the church tolerates sin.
   b. Without discipline, the church courts the possible loss of Christ's presence.
   c. both of the above

5. A church, lacking scriptural discipline bathed in prayer, eventually becomes
   a. a cutting edge church in the community.
   b. spiritually powerless and chaotic.
   c. socially acceptable.
   d. a praying church.
7. People fear that discipline will divide or possibly destroy the church. What really happens?
8. In what manner does Christ's withdrawal from the church take place?
9. Why do churches fail to rebuke sin with boldness?
10. How does God respond to church discipline?
11. What are the principal purposes of church discipline?
12. Faithfulness to Christ means death to self rather than compromise. Neutrality qualifies as
    a. the wise thing to do.
    b. something to be strongly considered.
    c. spiritual adultery.
    d. all of the above
13. In Exodus 34:14, what is the name given for God?
14. What is the goal of church discipline in relation to Christ?
15. Can you share an experience where you participated in positive church discipline?
16. How is church discipline an example of true worship?
17. What temptations should a congregation avoid before participating in church discipline?
18. Describe the character of a congregation that does not support church discipline.
19. Are you aware of situations within your congregation that should be subject to church discipline?
20. How can the principles related to church discipline be applied in a family situation?

*Exercises*
1. Pray that the Lord will convict you, your family, and your church of any sins that hinder your prayers. Pray that these

barriers will be removed by confession, reconciliation, and restitution.

2. Pray with your spouse or your family about a proper attitude toward discipline.

3. Discuss this book with your family and/or close prayer partners. Are you learning to pray with Christ obviously present and actively in charge?

4. If you have any questions about the prayer vision presented in this book, look at the last page to find out how to send your questions to the author.

# FIFTH KEY:

## BRINGING US INTO HARMONY WITH OUR FATHER IN HEAVEN

*That you may be filled with all the fullness of God. (Eph. 3:19)*

## CHAPTER TEN

# Becoming True Worshipers

THE POWER OF PRAYING together changes us into disciplined servants, and this change reaches its culmination when we share the mind and heart of the Savior as true worshipers. Our attitudes and conduct must be in harmony with our prayers, and our petitions must be in harmony with our high calling in Christ. We have been called to share the love of the Lord and to live in harmony with His love.

Worship is the highest form of prayer, and effective prayer is always in harmony with pure worship. Life is a symphony, and Christ is the Great Conductor. Just as all the instruments in the symphony must be in tune with the same pitch, so our spirit must be attuned to the Spirit of Christ. As all the players must wait on the conductor to start the concert and set the tempo, so we must all wait on the Lord to set the tempo of our steps.

Key five for effective prayer is to trust Christ to bring us into harmony with our heavenly Father. This requires not only that we unite in acts of real worship, but also that we take on the character of true worshipers. God is not seeking people who will worship Him for an hour on Sunday morning and then depart to live in another spirit the rest of the week. Rather, God is seeking worshipers who are devoted to Him only and thus keep their hearts exclusively for Him at all times.

Just as a spouse does not want a marriage partner who professes complete love and devotion and then habitually flirts with others, so God wants to occupy His exclusive place of love in our hearts always. Harmony with God is the highest aim of all effective prayer. This harmony can be shared by couples, families, small fellowship groups, and churches united in true worship. Christ is completely free to manifest His glorious presence, especially as He actively takes charge in such an environment.

In his book titled, *From Grace to Glory*, Murdoch Campbell tells of a godly Highland minister who was a true worshiper. However, he was married to a stubborn, self-willed wife.

He sat one day in his room reading his Bible. The door opened and his wife entered. Her hand snatched the book from him and threw it into the fire. He looked into her face and quietly remarked, "I never sat at a warmer fire." It was an answer that turned away her wrath and marked the beginning of a new and gracious life. His Jezebel became a Lydia. The thorn became a lily.[1]

This man had obviously dealt with the problem of sin at its very root. I'm not suggesting that he was sinless, but that his inner life was insulated from the sudden storms and pressures of this sin-cursed world. He reminds me of a certain spider who lives inside an air bubble under water. Though the creature is in the water, it is sealed off from it. We all need something like this, namely, a spiritual "bomb shelter" for our inner person. Most of us fail to find such a sanctuary because we only deal with surface sins and never come to grips with the root of all sin.

## The Root Issue

Is there a single issue of truth and righteousness that touches the fundamental root of all right and wrong? I believe there is. This basic issue is summed up in the first commandment, "You shall have no other gods before me" (Exod. 20:3). Or to state the injunction positively, "You shall worship the Lord your God, and Him only you shall serve" (Matt. 4:10).

We need to think deeply about the full meaning of this commandment. It is not only first and foremost, but it is also the sum and substance of our duty as God's people. If you are right here, you will be right all the way through. Because there is only one God, then all of one's duty is to Him alone. God must have an exclusive personal relationship with you that dominates and overshadows everything else in your life. This is the compelling reason why we must learn to do everything by prayer in order to enjoy the peace of God (Phil. 4:6–7).

To visualize this basic truth, picture yourself standing on earth and God in heaven. Now draw a line straight up from you to God. This is the trunk, or the relationship that governs all other relationships in life. Now draw a cross bar. This is the branch that goes from you to others. If you are treating God right, you will be right in your dealings with all people. The divine-human relationship is the great thermostat, regulator, or trunk line that controls people-to-people relationships.

Today, we desperately need to recover this truth, not only to find the secret of inner peace that the godly Highlander discovered, but also to save our families and ultimately our nation from ripping apart at the seams. Because we do not really see the full meaning of our trunk line relationship to God, we have lost all sense of order in the home.

Militant women's libbers charge that the family is just a trap led by tyrannical husbands who have deceived unsuspecting females into letting the male be the head. Even good Christians are sometimes fuzzy on the divine order of leadership and authority in the home, the church, and society in general. A husband's headship is a responsibility, not a license to do as he pleases.

Men are often guilty of demanding that their wives obey them, while they ignore their wife's heart cry, "Love me as Christ loves the church." Husbands also fail to humble themselves and lead their wives in shared mutual submission to God (Eph. 5:21). Wives need to hear their husbands praying that Christ will take charge of their marriage and lead them as a couple in complete submission to the Lord.

With the loss of order in the home, love has lost all meaning. Take, for example, the liberal seminary students who viewed films of gay life and exclaimed, "those homosexuals really love each other!" And how about the mother of six children who wrote "Dear Abby" that she had nothing against her husband, but since she had gotten involved with another man, she was ready to leave her family for the paramour because "this is my last chance for real love!"

I'm convinced that the first commandment holds the secret of inner peace that no storm can disturb. It gives order to all our personal relationships as well as definition, meaning, and reality to love. For that reason, I invite you to take a closer look at this basic commandment and consider its full meaning.

## Three Exclusive Claims

The exclusive personal relationship called for in the first commandment can be explained by looking at three exclusive claims that God makes upon us. Two of these are addressed to our inner person. First, we are to love God with all our heart, soul, and mind (Matt. 22:37–38). Second, we are to fix all our hopes and expectations in life on Him alone (Ps. 62:5–8). (Remember that love for God and fixing all our hopes and expectations on Him are the heartbeat of a healthy and powerful prayer life that is centered on Christ.) Third, every word we speak and every action we take must be said or done as a service to God alone (Col. 3:22–4:1). This third claim governs all our outward conduct.

## Love God with All Your Heart

One time in family devotions, my children thought that they had me stumped on the first claim mentioned above. They asked, "If you love God with *all* your heart, how do you have any love left for mother?" That was a good question! I had to send up a silent prayer for wisdom before I tried to answer it. Finally, I said, "My love for your mother, or anyone else for that matter, can only be a branch off of my love for God."

This truth explains why love for your neighbor is the second and subordinate commandment (Matt. 22:39). We are now brought face to face with the true nature of love. The only way you can love a great unlimited person like God is by obeying

Him. John wrote, "For this is the love of God, that we keep His commandments" (1 John 5:3). The apostle also said that the way we know we truly love the children of God is by loving the Lord and keeping His commandments (1 John 5:2).

If love is equated with obeying God, then love has a definite order. For example, when Jonathan surrendered to David all his claims to his father's throne, that was true, unconditional love, for God had decreed that David (not Jonathan) would take the throne after Saul. It would not have been love for David to insist that Jonathan keep his throne rights.

In the same manner, it is love for the wife to let her husband be her head, but it is sin to reverse that order. Some parents put their love for their children ahead of their love for their mate. This is wrong. If a couple really loves their children, they will put the husband-wife relationship first and the parent-child relationship second (Gen. 2:24).

Love also has a clearly defined meaning and character. Homosexual acts are sin, not love. A woman forsaking her family is leaving love behind. In fact, she will not find true love in adultery.

Love for your marriage partner is a unique form of intimacy and affection that cannot be shared with any other human being. Failure to give your child proper discipline is a sign of hatred, not love. The way to love lazy Christians (for example, those who refuse to work) is to tell them politely that you will no longer feed them (2 Thess. 3:5–12). How do you love a stubborn, rebellious brother who is living with his father's wife and refuses to forsake sin? Paul wrote that he should be committed to Satan for the destruction of the flesh so that his spirit might be saved in the end (1 Cor. 5:1–5).

Love is not the flimsy, flabby, gushy, spineless, characterless, and easygoing sentiment that folks sometimes imagine. Love is willingly obeying God and treating your fellow human being with kindness and generosity, even when it requires sacrifice.

Notice that we owe *all* our love to God. This is a key truth. The godly Highlander mentioned above must have understood this, for he treated his wicked wife with Christlike love, not because she deserved it, but because God deserved it. The husband's treatment of her was an expression of love to God. The Highlander gave all his love to God, and the wife benefited from the overflow.

## Trust God Only

How about trust? How is it possible to trust only God? Aren't we supposed to trust everyone else? In reality, the trust we place in others should be a subordinate part of our trust in God. "My soul, wait silently for God alone, for my expectation is from Him" (Ps. 62:5). This expresses nicely how all-inclusive should be our dependence on God.

Failure to trust only God can leave us feeling bitter. A minister who had passed through a deeply disturbing trial that left him badly shaken told me, "People let you down." Indeed, they do. But why did that disturb his soul's composure? Isn't it because he was not trusting only in God? All of our expectations and hopes in life must be fixed on God alone. That's why our trust in people should be subordinate to our hope in God.

When I went to a banker to borrow money to build a church, he did not want to loan money to our congregation because we had no credit record. He asked me to get a group of wealthy businessmen to co-sign the note. He made it perfectly plain that he was depending on those wealthy men to pay back the loan. He would loan us the money, but his trust was really in them. (We didn't borrow the money, but I'm sure you see the point.)

Human relations are built on trust as well as love. We trust each other when we share life in a church or in certain business associations. When a man and woman give themselves to each other in marriage, they completely place their whole life and happiness in one another's hands.

But your marriage partner is only human. Suppose he (or she) fails you? And what if your Ahab (or Jezebel) remains a thorn in the flesh all your life? John Wesley's wife did. Either you can become bitter or you can trust God to co-sign the note. If you trust God to co-sign the note, then He will see that the relationship works together for your good, even though others let you down. Incidentally, before you enter into a marriage or business partnership, it would be wise to ask God to "co-sign the note." But if you are already married to a "hard to live with" partner before you learned this truth, then trust God to meet your present need.

Our complete trust in God must undergird our trust in people. He promised to use even their evil for our eternal good, and His eternal reward makes all our love and trust worthwhile (Rom. 8:28; Gen. 50:20; 1 Cor. 15:58). Wait only on God. If you focus all your expectations on Him, you will never be disappointed.

## Serve God Only

Such love and trust insulate our heart in the midst of the stormy waters of life. Remember the spider in the air bubble? Armed with this insulation for our inner person, we are ready to serve only God (Matt. 4:10). Whatever we say or do to people should first be offered as a sacrificial service to God. We can become like the godly Highlander mentioned earlier who counted on God to do him good through his wife's rudeness. The husband, in turn, treated her with love and kindness for God's sake. That kind of life is similar to living in heaven on earth. It is simply out of this world, even though we are still in the world. It represents total commitment to God and separation from evil.

All of us want to live like that, but when the good news reached us we were already involved in all kinds of relationships that hinder such a life. Maybe you are saying, "I'm all for it, but I'm married to a very demanding husband (or wife), and you don't know Harry (or Sally)! I'm not free to serve only God." Or perhaps a tough, profane boss stands over you at the office. Every relationship we have in this fallen world can become extremely difficult. So you cry, "How are we going to get these people off our back so that we will be free to serve only God?"

The answer is found in Paul's words to first-century Christian slaves toiling under cruel, pagan masters (Col. 3:22–25). You start by taking your eyes off of the one on earth who is over you and look straight up to the Lord, who rules over all. Now remember this Lord once endured an unfair trial, suffered shame, and finally was crucified as a criminal. He endured all this for you (1 Peter 2:21–25).

Today, Jesus is asking you to fulfill your duties to those over you and around you as an expression of love for Him. "And whatever you do, do it heartily, as to the Lord and not to men" (Col. 3:23). Verse 24 reminds us that God promises to eternally reward us and that our only real boss is the Lord Jesus Christ. You serve people on orders from Christ and render to them the high quality of service that Christ deserves. Endure insult, ingratitude, and unfairness for Him who endured so much for you. You will one day be eternally rewarded, and they will get what they deserve.

Sometimes the situation is reversed, and you have to be a gracious boss to a contrary employee, or a nice husband to a mean wife, or an even-tempered parent to an ill-tempered child. Even in these instances we must respond in a godly manner as an expression of our love, faith, and commitment to the Lord.

For the dedicated believer, all of life is elevated to the level of divine service. At the kitchen sink, wash the dishes as a service only to God. Let this rule govern all that you say and do (Col. 3:17, 23). Then all your human relations will be enriched with the abundance of God's grace in your heart.

## How to Enter In

To enter into such a life calls for some definite steps that you must take now. First, you must make the decision to dedicate yourself wholly to the Lord because you love Him supremely (Rom. 12:1–2). This is a decision that affects the rest of your life. You will always be held accountable for it. I have hanging on the wall of my study a plaque painted by a friend that says,

"Oliver Price, bondslave of Jesus Christ." This is a total commitment to which I have bound myself forever. Take this step and you will experience Christ's power within you.

The second step is learning to cope with failure. Though we wholly trust the Lord for grace to fulfill our commitment to Him, our conscience (growing ever more tender) constantly pricks us because we fall short of such a high standard. Do not be disheartened. Confess your faults. Trust God to restore you, and thank the Spirit for faithfully alerting you to your sins. Remember how Jesus prayed for Peter and restored him after he had denied the Lord (Luke 22:31–32; John 21:15–19).

Third, I have found that it helps me to draw a little diagram like the one shown at the bottom of this page. Memorize and meditate on the verses that go with it and imagine that this is the place where your life is hidden with Christ in God. Constantly review these verses plus others in a similar fashion.

Fourth, memorize verses such as 1 Thessalonians 5:22–24, Hebrews 13:20–21, and Jude 24–25. Let these passages soak into your mind until you develop strong confidence that God has purposed to perfect your dedication to Him. Remember that He has sealed His eternal purposes for you with the blood of the everlasting covenant. "He who calls you is faithful, who also will do it" (1 Thess. 5:24).

Trust God only (Ps. 62:5–8). Fix all expectations on Him.

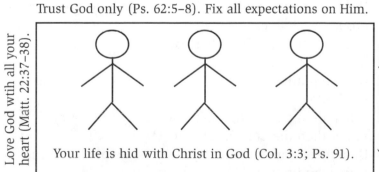

Love God wtih all your heart (Matt. 22:37–38).

Serve God only (Matt. 4:10; Col. 3:22–4:1).

Your life is hid with Christ in God (Col. 3:3; Ps. 91).

Give to God all of your personal rights (Phil. 2:5–8).

Fifth, if possible, meet in prayer with your spouse, your family, a small group, and even with your whole church. Share your commitment to become true worshipers. Invite them to join you in claiming the presence of Christ, especially as you unite in the power of praying together under His active headship. Trust Jesus to change you as He sees fit and to bring you into the heavenly harmony of true worshipers who serve Him alone. God's all-sufficient grace will renew you daily and lead you on the upward way to everlasting glory. Always remember that Christ is able to save you completely, for He ever lives to intercede for you (Heb. 7:25).

## Review Questions

1. Effective prayer is always in harmony with
   a. God's will?
   b. confessed sin?
   c. mature Christians?
   d. pure worship?
2. What is key five for effective prayer?
3. What is the highest aim of all effective prayer?
4. What is the single issue of truth and righteousness that touches the fundamental root of all right and wrong?
5. Which commandment holds the secret of inner peace that no storm can disturb?
6. What is the only way that you can love a great unlimited person like God?
7. What does it mean when a parent fails to give a child proper discipline?
8. If love is obeying God, then love has a definite
   a. price to pay?
   b. commitment?
   c. feeling?
9. What are many of the idols that Americans today turn to rather than the Lord Jesus Christ?
10. Underneath our trust in people must be our total trust in God, who promised

    a. to use even the evil of others for our good?

    b. to give us eternal reward?

    c. both of the above

11. Consider each of your major relationships. How do they compare to your relationship with Christ?

12. What are your hopes and expectations in life? Are they fixed on Christ alone?

13. Give one example of a sacrificial service to God.

14. Which activities have you participated in over the last week that were not considered a service to God?

15. What does enduring insult, ingratitude, and unfairness bring to you?

16. How can you show love to those around you?

17. For the dedicated believer, all of life is elevated to what level?

18. What is God's promise found in 1 Thessalonians 5:24?

19. Whom should you meet with for prayer, if possible, to become a true worshiper?

20. Consider your attitude during your weekly worship service. Is it an attitude of prayer and harmony with God? What about your attitude during the day? Is it an attitude of worship?

*Exercises*

1. Share with your close prayer partners, your spouse, and/ or your family your commitment to be a true worshiper. Ask for their help.

2. As you finish your day, review your activities, attitudes, and actions with God. Ask God to make known anything that you need to confess or change in the future.

## CHAPTER ELEVEN

# Offering the Sacrifice of Praise

PAUL REACHED A HIGH degree of harmony with God. The apostle's letter to the Philippians unveils the secret of his harmony with the Father. Paul's chief desire was for Christ to be magnified in his body no matter what the cost (Phil. 1:20). Consider the cry of the apostle's heart: "that I may know Him and the power of His resurrection, and the fellowship of His sufferings, being conformed to His death" (Phil. 3:10). Paul's prayers were powerful because they were free from selfishness.

Effective prayer seeks the presence of Christ and His active leadership so that we may share not only the blessings and joy of Christ but also His sufferings. We reach a high level of harmony with God when we offer the sacrifice of praise during our times of hardship. Some honored servants of God have shown us how to do this.

A poverty-stricken black pastor stood at desperation corner. Charles A. Tindley was serving a tiny, struggling church in Cape May, New Jersey. A blinding blizzard paralyzed the town. His baby had died in the cold, dark night. Dawn brought no sign of relief. All Mrs. Tindley could serve for breakfast was stale bread.

In his book entitled *Their Finest Hour*, author Charles Ludwig explains how Pastor Tindley met the crisis. "Set the table like we always do," he urged his wife. Courageously, he thanked God for his salvation, his health, and his children. The family listened and wondered. All of a sudden, someone knocked on the door. A brother in the Lord entered with his arms loaded with groceries. The storm had delayed his coming. Meanwhile, Charles Tindley had passed a severe test of faith with flying colors. Pastor Tindley, an ex-slave, went on to build a church in Philadelphia that ministered to thousands. Remarkably, a grandson of his former master was converted under his ministry![1]

This pastor's spirit of gratitude and praise thoroughly equipped him and served as the foundation for a life that God mightily used. Tindley learned the secret of releasing his faith through thankful praise. His faith soared into the highest heavens on the wings of humble gratitude. There he enjoyed the heights of intimate fellowship with God.

This same reality can transform our inner lives today, especially as we enter into the simple truth that *thanksgiving turns trials into blessings*. It can turn sour personalities into sweetness of spirit and frustration into gratitude. Most importantly, thankful praise brings all honor and glory to God the Father.

What exactly does "thankful praise" mean? Why do individuals, churches, and even nations rise and fall according to this concept? Thankful praise to God differs from words of appreciation to our fellow human beings. Unfortunately when we say, "Dear heavenly Father, thank You for this food," it comes out sounding more like, "Dear John, thank you for the birthday present you sent me." This type of appreciation will never free our faith.

## Biblical Thanksgiving: Step One

Psalm 100 provides three basic elements of thanksgiving that liberate our faith. First, thanksgiving is submission. The psalmist recognized that the Lord is God by saying, "Know that the LORD, He is God; it is He who has made us, and not we ourselves; we are His people and the sheep of His pasture" (v. 3). The Lord made us and holds absolute power over us. He exercises this power as a tender, loving shepherd for our own good. Therefore, we should submit to His will with gratitude.

Charles Tindley found this truth. He showed supreme trust in the Lord, his Shepherd. No matter how bare the table, he thanked God. This was real "grace" before the meal. This explains how he was ready to receive from God a powerful ministry. True grace before meals should mean, "I gratefully submit to the hand that feeds me." It has been well said, "Devote yourself to God, and you will find that God fights the battles of a will resigned."

A salty preacher once thrust an accusing finger at his congregation—who missed this basic lesson—and declared, "Why, any dumb ox or donkey would recognize the one who feeds them as their master! But you don't!" Not many preachers can get by with such hard-hitting language. But this one did! His name was Isaiah (Isa. 1:1–3). He never would have won a popularity contest, but God used him to tell the people of Judah why their nation would fall.

As a matter of fact, the whole human race fell for the same reason. Adam and Eve were filled with their own wisdom and self-sufficiency. Did they thank God before eating the forbidden fruit? Obviously not! Romans 1:21 traces humankind's depravity to the fact that "although they knew God, they did not glorify Him as God, nor were thankful."

John Noble suffered in a Communist prison. The jailers nearly starved him and his fellow prisoners to death. The Communists finally passed out old crusts of bread. While the other prisoners gobbled it down, John gratefully pondered each bite, thanking God for his meal. This decision literally saved his life. The prisoners who stuffed their starving stomachs all died, for eating so fast killed them. Noble sat in his cell, overwhelmed with praise to God, and slowly nibbled the crust of bread. The spirit in which he ate saved his life.

## Biblical Thanksgiving: Step Two

The second element of biblical thanksgiving is joy. Glum submission misses the point. As we enter God's gates with thanksgiving, we are to "make a joyful shout to the LORD" (Ps. 100:1). We must "come before His presence with singing" (v. 2). Paul and Silas knew heaven's joy as they sang in prison with their backs open with raw wounds from a severe beating (Acts 16:22–25).

Joyful thanksgiving is often an act of faith in the midst of life's tests. A few years ago, we struggled to make necessary repairs on our office. Nothing went right, and we could not accomplish the task. Our ministry suffered, and we could not attend to necessary details. My patience wore thin. I suffered discouragement under the burden of my circumstances.

One morning as I left for work, I told my wife, "I'm going to thank the Lord and enjoy the day regardless of whether we repair the office." At our office prayer meeting, I told the staff the same thing. Joyful thanksgiving marked our prayers. Before we finished praying, a volunteer—an expert repairman—showed up to help with the work. Please understand I don't always find relief that quickly. But I can always get "on top of my circumstances" by rejoicing and thanking God. It's only right to rejoice, for He controls all circumstances for my own good. God used my difficulties to release my faith through the joyful expression of thanks to Him.

Thankful praise transforms lives. It opens our hearts to God in such a way that we find freedom in our problems and can actually benefit from them. Let me explain how this works.

On one occasion, God took a family and unveiled His plan for their future. He made known that out of twelve brothers, the next to the youngest would lead them, and all of them would serve him. This so enraged the older brothers that they plotted his demise and eventually sold him into slavery. This brother suffered unjustly for years, yet profited from all his afflictions. His trials actually prepared him to serve as a kind, forgiving, and gracious ruler over a nation. But his brothers, eaten up with envy, jealousy, and guilty consciences, suffered from their self-inflicted torture all the more.

Why did Joseph benefit from his trials? He believed that God intended his afflictions for good (Gen. 50:20). Our own joyful submission rests on our confidence that the Lord, who controls all things, is good (Ps. 100:5) and that He makes all things work together for our eternal good (Rom. 8:28).

## Biblical Thanksgiving: Step Three

The third element of biblical thanksgiving is adoration. We read, "Enter into His gates with thanksgiving, and into His courts with praise. Be thankful to Him, and bless His name" (Ps. 100:4). We see here an attitude of praise and adoring wonder.

This was abundantly demonstrated to me by the late Mrs. Ethel Tylee, a former missionary, whom I knew early in my Christian life. She frequently prayed, "Blessed be the Lord God, the God of Israel, who only does wondrous things!" (Ps. 72:18). Coming from her, those words really meant something to me as a young teenager. While she was serving as a missionary in hostile territory in Brazil, her husband and only child were killed by Indians. She and her unborn child were left for dead. She escaped and later gave birth to her baby.

I heard Mrs. Tylee repeat Psalm 72:18 so many times that she indelibly etched it in my memory. She demonstrated something far beyond grateful submission and deep joy. She blessed and praised the King of kings with adoring wonder.

Many of us may do all right when it comes to submission and joy, but we fall short of worshiping the Lord with adoring praise. Our struggle to understand hardships that have befallen our friends, family, or ourselves hinder our worship of God. Trying to figure out what possible good could come from these difficulties places us on the journey to nowhere. We can't fathom the mystery of God's providence.

Adoration takes us beyond our understanding. On the wings of praise, we adore God beyond our mere comprehension. By faith, we affirm that God does not struggle to make the best of bad situations. He only does wondrous things through them and in spite of them.

Mrs. Tylee's adoring wonder exemplifies "the sacrifice of praise." Hebrews 13:15 calls us to make this sacrifice. "Therefore by [Jesus] let us continually offer the sacrifice of praise to God, that is, the fruit of our lips, giving thanks to His name." It has been well said that, "Praise becomes a sacrifice when we have to die to our own opinions to offer it. We give up our ideas of what is best in order to praise God for our trials. We trust Him even when we cannot understand His ways. By doing so, we die to self."

William Carey knew this "sacrifice of praise" when his printing plant burned to the ground, taking with it years of tedious translation work. He calmly spoke, "How unsearchable are God's ways! The Lord let this happen so that I might trust Him more. I will be still and know that He is God." When Christians in his native England heard about the fire, they rallied to Carey's aid more than ever. In the end, the benefit of the fire far surpassed the loss.

## The Ultimate Thanksgiving

God Himself offered the greatest sacrifice of praise and thanksgiving. Christ died as the sacrifice of thanksgiving prescribed in the law (Lev. 7:12). Christ Himself offered thanks for the bread and the cup at the Last Supper. They represented His body and blood, which He would soon offer as an atoning sacrifice for the sins of the world (John 1:29; 1 John 2:2).

Psalm 22:3 provides amazing insight into Christ's motivation in offering Himself as an atoning sacrifice. "But You are holy, enthroned in the praises of Israel." God is at home in the midst of the praises of His people. He communicates His obvious presence to His people and actively takes charge when they truly praise Him.

Praise and thanksgiving define the only way God and people can live happily together for all eternity. God can *impose* His unlimited wisdom and power upon us regardless of whether we want it. But He does not enjoy doing so. Instead, He desires our willing, adoring, joyful submission. At times, God does impose His divine wisdom and power on a grumbling person, or nation, or church. It grieves Him to do so. It's not done with joy.

As an adult, imagine yourself having to take an unwilling child to the doctor in order to save his life. Out of your superior wisdom and knowledge, you impose your will upon the child's and force this treatment upon him. You have to do so, but you do not enjoy it.

If the child would only trust you, what a change would take place! He would submit to you in a spirit of thankful praise. He might not understand, but he could look to your superior wisdom with adoring wonder. You could then enjoy each other. More than that, you would feel no reluctance in bringing to his life in many other situations all the wisdom and power that you are capable of providing.

The Lord desires to enthrone Himself in the hearts of people as the only wise and all-loving God. This describes the thrust of Scripture in totality. We must allow God the freedom to act according to His superior wisdom and power *without* having to impose Himself on a doubting, reluctant, even rebellious humanity. In this light, praise proves more important than supplication.

Are you ready to "blast off" into the orbit of continual, thankful praise? If so, here's the countdown. First, make every problem and every disagreeable person an occasion for prayer and praise. Second, count on God to use them for your own good. Third, lift off in faith. Thank and praise the Lord in adoring wonder without waiting to see the good in the midst of pain. Don't fret over trying to understand His grand scheme of things.

If you willingly do these things in faith, your flight will launch you into the heavens. You will soar to the heights of complete trust in God, and you will sing and worship the Lord with your heart. Your prayers will welcome Christ. A song of heavenly joy will fill your soul.

## Review Questions

1. What turns trials into blessings?
2. Do you agree with the following statement? Why or why not?

Individuals, even nations, rise and fall according to the concept of thankful praise.

3. According to Psalm 100, the first key that liberates our faith is which of the following:
   a. submission
   b. confession
   c. repentance
   d. happiness
4. What does true grace before a meal really mean?
5. How did Isaiah rebuke the lack of thankful praise?
   a. winning friends and influencing people
   b. telling people that they were dumber than an ox
   c. biblical preaching
   d. sending teams of young people to preach around the nation
6. What is the second element of biblical thanksgiving?
7. What is a little secret for "getting on top of your circumstances?"
   a. working a little harder
   b. maintaining a positive mental attitude
   c. seeing a counselor
   d. rejoicing and thanking God
8. How does thankful praise transform people?
9. Why did Joseph benefit from his trials?
10. What is the third element of biblical thanksgiving?
11. Praise becomes a sacrifice when
    a. we have to die to our own opinions to offer it?
    b. it comes at great personal cost?
    c. when no one knows about it?
    d. it is performed in private?
12. What is the supreme example of the sacrifice of praise?
13. God is at home in the midst of
    a. holy people?
    b. the praises of His people?
    c. grand and glorious music?
    d. powerful preaching?

14. Name the three ways to insure a life of continual, thankful praise.
15. What areas of your life, your family, or your church are not submitted to the kingship of Christ?
16. What situations have you recently experienced that are frustrating or difficult to understand?
17. Are you confident that God has control over these difficult situations? Why or why not?
18. In what ways can you be thankful for these difficult situations? In what ways are you still struggling to be thankful?
19. What are the attributes of God that could impact these difficult situations?
21. How would your trials be different if they were considered a blessing before they become a struggle?

*Exercises*

1. Offer a true prayer of thanksgiving—with submission, thanksgiving, and praise—at your family's next evening meal.
2. Meet with another church member to pray about one of the situations with which you struggle. Be sure to confess your submitted attitude, thanksgiving, and praise.

# CONCLUSION

*Jesus said to him, "I am the way, the truth, and the life. No one comes to the Father except through Me. (John 14:6)*

## CHAPTER TWELVE

# Dear God, How Can We Find You?

WHERE IS THE ONLY true and living God? Is He in all houses of worship or none of them? Many people in our society today don't believe that God dwells in any church or religious community. In fact, they think that you are an arrogant bigot if you claim that the God of Christians is the only true and living God. They would be blown away if they heard that our God and Savior meets with us and actively takes charge of us!

"The god of the Muslims is dead," proclaimed a missionary candidate to the Muslim world while speaking to a Bible-believing church. Three visitors reacted instantly, walking out angrily. With this gesture of contempt, we see the wave of the future, namely, that multiculturalism is in. Our society exalts tolerance of other religions and other morals as the supreme virtue.

Supposedly, you must not say that Christ is the only way to God. Nor can you find anything wrong with sodomy. You can have your religion and your morals, but don't you dare say other religions or "morals" are wrong!

On May 31, 1997, *The Dallas Morning News* reported in its religion section about Dr. Lonnie Kliever's class on world religions at Southern Methodist University. According to the *News*, he stated, "If I have a mission as a professor, it's to make the world safe for diversity." In the article, Dr. Kliever presents two models of truth—the probabilistic model and the mathematical model:

The mathematical posits truth as an "either-or" propo-
sition: "Billy Graham was using that model when he
said: 'Truth is intolerant. Two plus two equals four; it
doesn't equal five or three.'" The probabilistic model,
on the other hand, says that absolute, conclusive truth
cannot be known.[1]

All of the students quoted in the paper agreed that religious
truth is only probable. There is no absolute certainty. One student, who is a Sunday school teacher in a conservative, Bible-
preaching church, reportedly said, "Although I am a Christian,
I do not feel that other religions are wrong. I understand that
Christianity is not for everyone." Another agreed "that other
faiths are not completely off base. They're not wrong, but they
have a little farther to go—they miss the mark a little."

Not one student was cited who stood firmly with Christ. Yet
He declared, "I am the way, the truth, and the life. No one comes
to the Father except through me" (John 14:6). No mention was
made of the commandment, "You shall have no other gods before Me" (Exod. 20:3). Clearly, the Bible leaves no room for
people to claim that they are Christians and yet allow for the
possibility that other religions and other gods may be valid.

One student asserted, "I do not believe in any universal and
ultimate truths, except one, namely, that there is no ultimate
truth!" Our American society has bought into that deception in
alarming numbers. Public education, the media, movies, art, the
Supreme Court, and the business world operate on the assump-
tion that ultimate truth is a myth and that one true and living
God simply does not exist. The world promotes an agenda of
supreme tolerance. People think that the only hope of saving
our world from self-destruction is through the tolerance of all
religions, all morals, atheism, and no morals at all. To them tolerance means agreeing that all religions and all "morals" are
equally valid. Consequently belief in any God or religion is a
private matter for one's own personal comfort. Supposedly, religion and morals have no place in public life.

Our political system assigns God, religion, character, and morals to the place of total irrelevancy. "It's the economy, stupid!" "Money talks, and money is all that matters!" In the midst of this chaos, can we find hope? Indeed, we can!

## Finding Hope in the Midst of Chaos

Where would you go to discover the only true and living God, who is enthroned in the midst of His people, actively taking charge of them? In the Old Testament, seekers of God had an obvious clue as to where He lived and was enthroned. They just looked for the temple in Jerusalem. Some believe that the sanctuary had a unique, bright, and vertical supernatural cloud hovering over it. It has been called "the glory cloud." It signified God's presence in the temple, enthroned in the holy of holies.

The glory cloud had a notable history in Israel. In the Exodus this cloud stood between Israel and the attacking army of Egypt while the Hebrew people made their escape. To Israel, the cloud was like a huge floodlight illumining their way. To the Egyptians, it resembled a shield of darkness, hindering their march. This cloud led Israel through the wilderness. When the cloud moved, Israel moved. When the cloud stopped, they pitched their tents and planned to stay awhile. This was no ordinary cloud, but rather, it was a manifestation of the Lord's glorious presence among His people (Exod. 40:34–38).

By Daniel's day, things had drastically changed, for the glory of the Lord had withdrawn from the temple. The Babylonian army invaded Judah, destroyed Jerusalem and the temple, and carried thousands of Jews into captivity. However, the Bible makes it clear that God Himself gave His temple over to King Nebuchadnezzar's invading army. "And the Lord gave Jehoiakim king of Judah into his hand, with some of the articles of the house of God, which he carried into the land of Shinar to the house of his god; and he brought the articles into the treasure house of his god" (Dan. 1:2).

Just imagine how humiliating this was to the Jews! Holy

vessels from their temple lay as trophies at the feet of a lifeless pagan idol! What did the invaders think? Obviously, they assumed that the God of the Jews had been defeated. They thus had no apparent reason to fear Him. The ancient world knew the Lord's reputation as the God of the Jews. After all, He defeated Pharaoh, the mighty king of Egypt. He routed the Midianites with a tiny army of only three hundred led by Gideon. God destroyed a huge army of Assyrians under Sennacherib in answer to Hezekiah's prayers. These powerful acts were well known. The God of the Jews had repeatedly shown the world that He outclassed their pagan deities beyond comparison.

But now, at last, a foreign army had defeated the Jews. The enemy carried vessels from the temple of the Lord and laid them at the feet of an idol so the whole world would know that the God of the Jews had finally been defeated. Daniel and his three friends were among the thousands of Jewish captives carried away by the Babylonians. In general, the captives viewed the faith of their ancestors as bankrupt, which left them in defeat and despair. In reality, religion in Judah had been sliding downhill for centuries. Now it had finally bottomed out. The religious community could hardly sink any lower.

What could devout Jews tell their children? The account of Moses and the Exodus would have a hollow ring. It would sound more like religious folklore than history to a generation seeing so much hypocrisy and no intervention from God to rescue His people, as He had done in days of old.

The account of the Exodus would raise some extremely embarrassing questions. Why didn't God defeat the wicked Babylonians as He had the Egyptians? Why did He allow the enemy to take holy vessels from His temple and carry them off to Babylon? Why were God's people in captivity to pagan masters like their ancestors had been to Pharaoh? Where was their God, especially now that His glory had departed from the temple? Did these tragedies mean that their religion was no longer valid?

The Jewish faith faced questions similar to those Christianity faces in our country today. Many who profess belief in Christ are not prepared to give unbelievers convincing proof that Jesus is the only way to the Father. Too many conclude that perhaps the God of the Bible is not the only true deity. They have exchanged certainty for probability and a tolerance of all gods.

Christians who sing like believers on Sunday and behave like unbelievers the rest of the week must number in the vast multitudes. As mentioned earlier, a Gallup poll concluded, "In ethical behavior, there is very little difference between the churched and unchurched."[2]

In his day, Elijah demanded of God's people, "How long will you falter between two opinions? If the Lord is God, follow Him" (1 Kings 18:21). The only true, living, and almighty God could not coexist with other so-called gods. Elijah was a man of prayer, and his petitions led to a showdown, forcing the Hebrew people to get off the fence of indecision. The prophet wanted them to come down firmly on the side of the Lord, rather than worship Baal. The living and true God demanded that His people serve only Him.

Christians in America today must face the same choice. We can learn a lesson from Daniel, who wholly devoted himself to God in one of the darkest hours of the Jewish faith. Daniel knew that his God was still the only sovereign, the King of Kings and Lord of Lords. Furthermore, Daniel was ready to risk his life to trust and obey the God of Israel.

Daniel and his three friends—Shadrach, Meshach, and Abed-Nego—show us the crucial role of prayer in times such as these. When God answered their prayers, it gave Jews and Gentiles alike undeniable evidence of almighty God's universal presence and eternal power. God was neither dead nor defeated. He was looking for obedient, praying believers through whom He could convince the whole world that He alone reigns as the only true and living Lord. It is to Him that the King of Babylon and all humankind had to bow in humble submission. Working in prayer partnership with Daniel and his three friends, God distinguished Himself from all other gods and their deluded followers.

God didn't need a large crowd. He just needed a few believers who were completely loyal to Him. Daniel and his three friends proved to God that they measured up. They were ready to face the ultimate test of loyalty to God, namely, death itself.

## Leading Up to the Ultimate Test

The test came when Daniel and his friends were chosen to serve King Nebuchadnezzar and him only! The official appointed over them changed their names. They arrived in Babylon with names honoring the God of Israel but their new names honored the gods of Babylon. These Jews were expected to forget their heritage and their God. They had to learn to behave like idolatrous Babylonians.

For example, Daniel and his friends were ordered to eat meat that had not been prepared in accordance with the law of Moses. Plus, it had been offered to a pagan deity. Exodus 34:15 clearly forbade God's people from eating this kind of meat, but refusing to eat it could have cost the Jewish captives their lives.

Nevertheless, Daniel had purposed in his heart not to defile himself with the king's delicacies. He asked the official to excuse him and his three friends. The official feared for his own life, especially if he did not follow the king's orders. Daniel pled, "Please test your servants for ten days, and let them give us vegetables to eat and water to drink" (Dan. 1:12). At the end of ten days, they looked healthier than those who ate the king's food. On the final exam before the king, Daniel, Shadrach, Meshach, and Abed-Nego came out at the head of the class.

God had already tested and proven His followers. He knew that they were ready to love, honor, and obey Him no matter what the cost. So now He created an opportunity for the whole world to see that He alone is the only true God. Nebuchadnezzar had a dream and demanded that his magicians, astrologers, and sorcerers tell him two impossible details—what he dreamed and its interpretation. They were beside themselves with anguish and fear. The king was ready to execute them because they failed to meet his demand.

When the news reached Daniel, he asked for an opportunity to tell Nebuchadnezzar the dream and its interpretation. The risk was high. If Daniel failed, it meant torture and certain death. But Daniel knew that he could count on God. Daniel and his friends went to prayer concerning this dream. God revealed the secret to Daniel in a vision in the night. The next day, he went before the king and told him both what he had dreamed and its interpretation. Daniel explained that God had revealed these things to him. No other god had been able to do this.

The astonished king exclaimed, "Truly your God is the God of gods, the Lord of kings, and a revealer of secrets, since you could reveal this secret" (Dan. 2:47). As a result, Daniel and his friends received appointments to high offices in the kingdom. God had found His faithful followers. He worked through their prayers to give evidence to the king and the whole empire that He is the only true and living God.

Idolatry, however, doesn't die easily. The worst tests were yet to come for this brave band of godly young Jews. The king made a great image that exalted him and his great empire. Officials from all over the realm were ordered to attend the dedication of this image. At the sound of the music, all were expected to bow down and worship the idol.

Daniel evidently was away on some urgent business. But his three friends attended the ceremony and refused to bow down and worship, even after the king had summoned them and personally demanded that they fall prostrate before the image. Because of their insubordination, they were thrown into the furnace with heat so intense that it killed the soldiers who had hurled them in.

Amazingly, Daniel's three friends walked around safely in the red-hot furnace, and they were accompanied by a fourth man who was like "the Son of God" (Dan. 3:25). King Nebuchadnezzar went near the mouth of the fiery furnace and directed the young Jews to come out. Their hair was not even singed, nor was the smell of fire upon them (v. 27)!

The God of the Bible had given astonishing proof of His

supreme power over all the forces of people and nature. All the officials of the whole empire who had assembled witnessed this miraculous intervention of God. Subsequently, they carried this news back to every province of the vast empire, along with this official decree from King Nebuchadnezzar:

> Blessed be the God of Shadrach, Meshach, and Abed-Nego, who sent His Angel and delivered His servants who trusted in Him, and they have frustrated the king's word, and yielded their bodies, that they should not serve nor worship any god except their own God! Therefore I make a decree that any people, nation, or language which speaks anything amiss against the God of Shadrach, Meshach, and Abed-Nego shall be cut in pieces, and their houses shall be made an ash heap; because there is no other God who can deliver like this. (Dan. 3:28–29)

Through the loyal obedience and faith of these young Jews, God received universal acclaim as the supreme ruler. Their love for God proved so great that they were willing to die rather than disobey Him.

## Results of Faithfulness to God

Nebuchadnezzar saw the unique greatness of the God of the Jews. Still, the king's pride had yet to be conquered, for he exalted himself above God. Through Daniel, God warned Nebuchadnezzar to humble himself. Unfortunately, he quickly forgot and went about his arrogant way. One day while musing over his greatness and taking credit for the majesty of his kingdom, Nebuchadnezzar was stricken with complete insanity. Seven years later, he came to his senses and composed one of the strongest statements on the sovereignty of God ever written. The king sent this message throughout his empire:

> At the end of the time I, Nebuchadnezzar, lifted my eyes to heaven, and my understanding returned to me; and I blessed the Most High and praised and honored Him who lives forever: for His dominion is an everlasting dominion, and His kingdom is from generation to generation. All the inhabitants of the earth are reputed as nothing; He does according to His will in the army of heaven and among the inhabitants of the earth. No one can restrain His hand or say to Him, "What have You done?" (Dan. 4:34–35)

Some think that Nebuchadnezzar became a true believer in Daniel's God at this time. Regardless of whether this is so, the vast Babylonian Empire received a powerful witness that the God of the Bible is indeed is the only true and living God.

God chose Israel as His instrument to receive His special love and to be His witness to the whole world. The Israelites were to demonstrate that the Lord of the Bible is the only true and living God and there is no other (Deut. 6:4; Isa. 44:8; 45:5–6, 18, 22; 46:9). Tragically, the people as a whole failed to fulfill their mission. Nevertheless, it was fulfilled through Daniel and his dedicated friends.

God was no longer dwelling in the fallen Jerusalem temple, but He was manifested in the lives of Daniel and his three friends. God revealed Himself to the world through their unwavering testimony. God displayed His glory when He proved that He alone is God and that Daniel and his three friends were His true servants. They prepared for these tests when they purposed not to defile themselves with the king's meat (Dan. 1:8). Out of loyalty to their God, they separated themselves from the pagan culture in which they lived as captives. Their separation liberated their heart and conscience, and freed their spirit to serve God no matter what the cost.

## To God Be the Glory Today

Through those who unite in prayer, the Lord can once again in our day receive the glory due Him as the only true and living God. As His prayer warriors, we should abide in His presence under His active leadership and direction. Like Daniel and his three friends we must give the Lord our complete love, faith, and obedience, and let Him use us as He pleases to reveal Himself to the world. God can set the stage for the manifestation of His presence and power in an unbelieving world, but He must have prayer warriors who are ready to make the supreme sacrifice.

God appeals to the church today to come out and be separate from the pagan society in which we live, for as an assembly we are "the temple of the living God" (2 Cor. 6:16). If we will separate from the pagan world, God promised: "I will dwell in them and walk among them. I will be their God, and they shall be My people." Enjoying and experiencing God's presence among us is only possible when we maintain personal and congregational holiness. If we will live holy lives—namely, ones that are set apart in complete devotion to Him—He will demonstrate before the watching world that He is indeed the almighty Father and that we are His children (v. 17).

The Corinthian church needed to separate themselves from the pagan society of their city so that God could show Himself as their almighty Father. God is always the Father *of* His children, but He cannot be a Father *to* us as long as we fail to separate ourselves *unto* Him as our only God. In the parable of the prodigal son, the dad was always the father *of* his son, but when his son alienated himself and strayed far from home, the saddened parent could not be a father *to* him. When the young man returned, his dad was once again able to be a father *to* him and honor him as his son.

Our world today desperately needs to see the convincing evidence that we serve the only true and living God. Long ago Moses saw that the obvious presence of God actively in charge of Israel was essential. God had withdrawn from their camp and said that

He would not go with them to take possession of the promised land (Exod. 33:1–7). Moses saw the seriousness of this situation.

Moses also realized that God's withdrawal meant that Israel had broken her covenant with the Lord! God's presence, marked by the glory cloud, was what really separated Israel from the pagan nations. That is why Moses pled with God, "If Your presence does not go with us, do not bring us up from here. For how then will it be known that Your people and I have found grace in Your sight, except You go with us? So we shall be separate, Your people and I, from all the people who are upon the face of the earth" (Exod. 33:15–17). God heard Moses' prayer and promised to accompany the Israelites.

It is just as important today for Christ to be obviously present and actively in charge of our churches. His presence separates the Christian assembly from the world. Jesus' leadership alone can work mightily through us to convince the world that He is the only God and Savior and that we are His servants.

The sad truth is that Christ's leadership is largely ignored today. A. W. Tozer said it forcefully when he wrote that Christ has less actual authority in the average gospel church than a young pastor fresh out of seminary serving his first congregation.[3]

The only way to escape the ruin of our fallen pagan society is for us to unite in prayer. We must practice the power of praying together. We must commit ourselves to know and obey Christ as our only God and Savior. Christ alone can bind us together as one supernatural body under His headship. The goal is for us to become a new kind of community, one that is available for His use. Through His sovereign lordship over our lives, we seek to convince the unsaved that they must trust in Him or perish forever.

A mission society used an advertisement in a Christian magazine to bring into sharp focus the need to be set apart for service to God. The picture of four people with their hands clasped in prayer contained the caption: "Before we can reach the world, we have to be committed to reaching God." Then it explained, "Worship is where our mission begins."[4]

True corporate worship enthrones God in the midst of the worshipers (Rev. 4:2–11). The worshipers recognize God's right to rule. They honor His wisdom, power, and authority. They declare that He is worthy to reign. Thus, they open their hearts to Him and welcome His rule of love and grace. Worshipers depend on God for everything and express this dependence in prayer (Phil. 4:6–7).

The church began as a prayer meeting (Acts 1:14). The disciples dealt with the threat of persecution by prayerfully committing to witness for Christ no matter what the cost (Acts 4:23–35). The greatest missionary ministry of all time began in a worship service (Acts 13:1–5). Threats of church splits were resolved with the wisdom that God gave praying leaders (Acts 6:1–6; 15:1–29). The church in Acts knew how to find and keep their unity in the presence of the Holy Spirit and under His immediate lordship (Acts 15:28).

We must convince the world that our Lord is the only true and living God and that He dwells in the midst of our church, as He promised (Eph. 2:18–22; 2 Cor. 6:14–7:1). To accomplish this, we must practice as Richard Foster put it, "the reality and practicality of business decisions through Spirit rule."[5] He added, "Business meetings should be viewed as worship services."[6]

Foster told of visiting a business meeting attended by two hundred people who were debating an issue on which they held sharp differences of opinion. All of them truly wanted to know and do the will of God. Eventually, a united sense of God's direction began to take shape. However, a few people were not in agreement with the majority.

At this point, one person stood and said, "I do not feel right about this course of action, but I hope that the rest of you will love me enough to labor with me until I have the same sense of God's leading as the rest of you or until God opens another way to us."[7] All over the auditorium, little groups gathered "to share, to listen, to pray." After a time, they reached unity in the decision that they were facing.[8]

If your church does not have the vision of uniting in prayer, and of seeking Christ's presence and active leadership, don't criticize it or hastily leave it. Talk to your pastor and church leaders. With their approval, begin a prayer group that will seek Christ's active headship in your church. Discover the power of praying together. As you do this, wait humbly, patiently, and expectantly. God touched an empire through the prayers of four men, namely, Daniel, Shadrach, Meshach, and Abed-Nego. The Lord can also touch and bless your church. Like these four devout Jews, you can bloom where you are planted.

## Review Questions

1. In the Old Testament, how did seekers of God find Him?
2. By Daniel's day, what happened to God's presence in the temple?
3. When the pagan Babylonians defeated Israel, what did the enemy perceive concerning God?
4. After Israel's captivity, the account of the Exodus raised some extremely embarrassing questions. Name two.
5. According to Daniel 1, what was the ultimate secret of Daniel's success?
6. When Daniel asked for an appointment with the king, was this *before* or *after* receiving the vision?
7. How did the Lord give evidence to Nebuchadnezzar and the whole Babylonian empire that He is the only true and living God?
8. When the Israelites failed to fulfill their mission, how then did God work?
9. If God was no longer dwelling in the destroyed Jerusalem temple, where was He obviously present and actively in charge?
10. Share an experience in which you were aware of God's presence.
11. What are some commonly held pagan beliefs found in society regarding God?
12. How are your beliefs in God different from that of the unsaved?

13. Permeating society is the philosophy that says
    a. there is no universal and ultimate truth?
    b. there is no simple truth?
    c. truth is relative?
    d. truth is found in the eyes of the beholder?
14. In our age of rampant multiculturalism, many "Christians" conclude that
    a. tolerance (accepting all religions as valid) must be a good thing.
    b. morality is subjective.
    c. our God is not the only God.
    d. probability and tolerance should be exchanged for certainty.
15. God can set the stage for the revelation of His power to an unbelieving world, but
    a. He must have prayer warriors.
    b. He must have prayer warriors who are ready to make the supreme sacrifice.
    c. we must be willing to deliver God's message.
    d. we must be fully committed.
    e. all of the above
16. Why has the church lost power?
17. The church must convince the world that
    a. our Lord is the only true and living God?
    b. God dwells in the midst of the church, as He promised He would?
    c. both
    d. it is not our responsibility to convince anybody of anything?
18. What do you or your family need to change before God can use you to change the world's view of God?
19. What does your church need to change before God can use it to change the world's view of Him?
20. How do the prayers you participate in seek to make God known?

*Exercises*

1. Meet with a member of your church to pray for God to make Himself known to the world through you and your congregation.
2. Participate in your church's prayer meeting (or speak with your pastor about starting a prayer meeting) and share the vision of uniting in prayer to seek Christ's presence and active leadership.
3. Look at the last page of this book for the address to write to for further study on this subject.

# Endnotes

## Chapter 1

1. Mark Bubeck, *Raising Lambs Among Wolves* (Chicago: Moody, 1997), 11.
2. George Gallup, "George Gallup Looks at Religion in America," *RTS Ministry* 11, no. 2 (summer 1992): 10.
3. Ibid.
4. Richard Owen Roberts, *Revival Commentary, Revival Terminology in History* 1, no. 1 (summer 1996): 4.
5. Margaret M. Poloma and George H. Gallup Jr., *Varieties of Prayer: A Survey Report* (Philadelphia: Trinity, 1992), 131.
6. Ibid.
7. O. Hallesby, *Prayer* (Minneapolis: Augsburg, 1941), 11.
8. Ibid., 12.
9. "Why We Pray," *Life Magazine*, March 1994, 54.
10. Poloma and Gallup, *Varieties of Prayer: A Survey Report*, 1.
11. Ibid., 23.
12. Armin R. Gesswein, *With One Accord in One Place* (Harrisburg, Pa.: Christian Publications, 1978), 13.
13. Jules Ostrander, "God Comes to Nebraska Panhandle," *Revival Fellowship News*, fall 1990, 2.
14. Todd Mikkelson, "Revival Comes to Alliance," *The Evangelical Beacon*, January 1991, 9–10.
15. Michael Ullrich, "Small Town Transformed After Surprise Revival," *Moody Magazine*, July–August 1990, 66.
16. Ibid.
17. Ostrander, "God Comes to Nebraska Panhandle," 2.

18. Mikkelson, "Revival Comes to Alliance," 9.
19. Ullrich, "Small Town Transformed After Surprise Revival," 66.
20. Mikkelson, "Revival Comes to Alliance," 10.

## Chapter 2

1. Raymond Ortlund, *Let the Church Be the Church* (Waco, Tex.: Word, 1983), 33.
2. Armin R. Gesswein, *With One Accord in One Place* (Harrisburg, Pa.: Christian Publications, 1978), 7.
3. Ibid., 10.
4. Ibid., 92.
5. Ibid., 92–93.
6. Jonathan Edwards, *A Faithful Narrative of the Surprising Work of God* (Grand Rapids: Baker, 1979), 10.
7. Ibid., 14.
8. Ibid., 15.
9. Ibid.
10. Ibid., 17.
11. Ibid., 18.
12. Earle E. Cairns, *An Endless Line of Splendor* (Wheaton: Tyndale, 1972), 41.
13. Ibid., 42.
14. Ibid., 48.
15. Ibid., 48–49.
16. Ibid., 48.
17. Ibid.

## Chapter 3

1. Adapted from C. John Miller, *Outgrowing the Ingrown Church* (Grand Rapids: Zondervan, 1986), 94–97.
2. Condensed from A. J. Gordon, *How Christ Came to Church: The Pastor's Dream. A Spiritual Autobiography* (Philadelphia: American Baptist Publication Society, 1895).

## Chapter 4

1. C. I. Scofield, *The New Scofield Reference Bible* (New York: Oxford University Press, 1967), 1148.

## Chapter 6

1. Joseph M. Stowell, "Closed for Inventory," *Moody Magazine,* May 1988, 4.
2. William O. Douglas, *Points of Rebellion* (New York: Random House, 1969), 3.
3. Ibid., 88–89.
4. Dallas Willard, "Discipleship: For Super-Christians Only?" *Christianity Today,* 10 October 1980, 27.
5. Ibid.
6. Ed Dayton, *Whatever Happened to Commitment?* (Grand Rapids: Zondervan, 1984), 141.
7. Ibid., 129.
8. Erwin W. Lutzer, *Flames of Freedom* (Chicago: Moody, 1977), 27.
9. Kurt E. Koch, *Revival Fires in Canada* (Grand Rapids: Baker, 1975), 29.
10. Lutzer, *Flames of Freedom,* 33.
11. Ibid., 34.
12. Koch, *Revival Fires in Canada,* 35.
13. Ibid., 27.
14. Andrew Murray, *The Best of Andrew Murray* (Grand Rapids: Baker, 1978), 13.

## Chapter 7

1. Edwin Orr, *The Fervent Prayer: The Worldwide Impact of the Great Awakening of 1858* (Chicago: Moody, 1974), 16.
2. Ibid., 19.
3. Ibid., 17.
4. Ibid., 13.

## Chapter 8

1. Joseph Henry Thayer, *Greek-English Lexicon of the New Testament.* Corrected Ed. (New York: Harper & Brother, 1889), 405–6.
2. Warren W. Wiersbe, *The Integrity Crisis* (Nashville, Tenn.: Oliver Nelson, 1988), 17–18.
3. Adapted from "Synopsis of Revival with Life Action Ministries Team October 9–November 20, 1988," by Miles Seaborn. Used with his permission.

## Chapter 9

1. Roy E. Knuteson, *Calling the Church to Discipline* (Nashville, Tenn.: Action, 1977), 15.
2. Howard G. Hendricks, *Say It with Love* (Wheaton, Ill.: Victor, 1972), 59.
3. Marlin Jeshke, *Discipling the Brother* (Scottsdale, Pa.: Herald, 1972), 76.
4. Knuteson, *Calling the Church to Discipline*, 85.

## Chapter 10

1. Murdoch Campbell, *From Grace to Glory* (London: Banner of Truth Trust, 1970), 149.

## Chapter 11

1. Charles Ludwig, *Their Finest Hour* (Elgin, Ill.: David C. Cook, 1974), 18–19.

## Chapter 12

1. Mary A. Jacobs, *The Dallas Morning News,* Religion Section, 31 May 1997, 3G.
2. George Gallup, "George Gallup Looks at Religion in America," *RTS Ministry* 11, no. 2 (summer 1992): 10.
3. A. W. Tozer, "The Waning Authority of Christ in the Churches" (Harrisburg, Pa.: Christian Publications, n.d.), pamphlet.
4. Raymond C. Ortlund, "The First Business of God's People,"

Part 2 of "A Biblical Philosophy of Ministry," *Bibliotheca Sacra* 138, no. 550 (April–June 1981): 17–18.

5. Richard Foster, *Celebration of Discipline* (San Francisco: Harper, 1988), 184.

6. Ibid., 182.

7. Ibid.

8. Ibid.

**FOR MORE INFORMATION OR ANSWERS TO YOUR QUESTIONS** on praying together with Christ in charge, you may visit Bible Prayer Fellowship at www.praywithChrist.org or contact the author, Oliver W. Price, by mail: P.O. Box 810718, Dallas, TX 75381; e-mail: info@praywithChrist.org; fax: 972-241-1957; or phone: 972-241-6971.

**BIBLE PRAYER FELLOWSHIP** was created to challenge and mentor pastors, church leaders, and concerned Christians in a strategically focused prayer ministry for ongoing spiritual awakening in the home, church, and nation. We seek to call families and churches back to Christ-centered, Bible-based prayer. Realizing the necessity of unity both with God and with one another, in order to have a convincing testimony before the world (1 John 17:20–23), Bible Prayer Fellowship has resolved to focus its ministry on this challenge to unity and prayer.

We seek to fulfill our mission through

1. Our world wide web site (www.praywithChrist.org), which includes daily Bible prayers, our *Leader's Guide for Praying with Christ Present and Actively in Charge: Forgotten Secrets to a Live Prayer Meeting;* many articles on life-changing prayer; and new information that is added frequently.
2. Producing and distributing instructional written materials and audio tapes. These include:
   • Books and manuals for studying and teaching prayer.
   • Monthly mailings that deal with prayer.
   • Literature on prayer and revival from other sources.
   • Cassette tape messages on prayer and revival.
3. Conducting prayer seminars and preaching on prayer.
4. Airing "God Save America" radio spots—calling for prayer and spiritual awakening—on Christian radio stations across America.
5. Encouraging reading of the Bible through free distribution of Bibles, New Testaments, and gospel booklets.

Write us for a free subscription to our monthly *Revival Insights* and *Faith Partner* letters and for a list of cassettes on prayer and revival by Erwin Lutzer, Bill McLeod, Lou Sutera, Sammy Tippit, Joe Humrichous, Mark Bubeck, Jim Logan, and others.